Adventist Churches That Make a
DIFFERENCE

MAY-ELLEN and GASPAR COLÓN

Pacific Press®
Publishing Association

Nampa, Idaho | Oshawa, Ontario, Canada
www.pacificpress.com

Cover illustration from Lars Justinen
Interior design by Aaron Troia

The authors assume full responsibility for the accuracy of all facts and quotations as cited in this book.

You can obtain additional copies of this book by calling toll-free 1-800-765-6955 or by visiting http://www.AdventistBookCenter.com.

Library of Congress Cataloging-in-Publication Data
Colon, May-Ellen Netten, 1949-
  Adventist churches that make a difference / May-Ellen and Gaspar Colon.
    pages cm
  ISBN 978-0-8163-5896-0 (pbk.)
  1. Church work—General Conference of Seventh-Day Adventists. I. Title.
  BX6154.C58 2016
  286.7'3—dc23
                        2015034906

June 2016

Dedication

We dedicate this book to Monte Sahlin, our mentor and inspiration to promote and practice the ministry method of Jesus.

Contents

Introduction

"We wish there were a book that portrays *Adventist* churches that are making differences in their communities," a group of church members told us. They had just read the landmark book *Churches That Make a Difference*: *Reaching Your Community With Good News and Good Works*, by Ronald J. Sider, Philip N. Olson, and Heidi Rolland Unruh.[1] Within the book's solid biblical and practical content, the authors have woven stories of churches from many Christian denominations that are powerfully impacting their communities.[2] But no Adventist churches are mentioned. This can be taken as a challenge to Adventist churches to be missional churches that wholistically transform their communities for the better, as many other faith groups are doing.

The book you hold in your hands will highlight various Adventist churches and church-based nonprofit organizations and community projects around the world that are making differences in their communities.[3] Jesus' ministry was wholistic, restoring people physically, mentally, spiritually, and socially. His church is called to do the same. The stories are interspersed with material that will equip *your* church to carry out more effectively Jesus' ministry method of reaching people through socializing, sympathizing, and serving (Matthew 9:35, 36).[4]

We pray that this book will truly make a difference in your life and in your community or neighborhood as you read about powerful biblical foundations, principles, tools, and real-life examples that will activate your church to be salt and light (Matthew 5:13–16)—effective change agents—in Jesus' name! The world waits.

---

1. Ronald J. Sidler, Philip N. Olson, and Heidi Rolland Unruh, *Churches That Make a Difference: Reaching Your Community With Good News and Good Works* (Grand Rapids, MI: Baker Books, 2002).

2. The word *community* or *communities* could mean the internal community or congregation in the church, or it could mean the group of people outside the church—the neighborhood or region where the church serves. Unless stated otherwise, the latter definition will be used in this book.

3. An additional book could be written with powerful stories of how more than 600 Adventist hospitals, clinics, and dispensaries worldwide are making a difference by following Christ's ministry method. Another book could be written with stories from more than 7,579 (2013 statistics) Adventist schools that are impacting their communities wholistically. Great potential and reality for making a difference!

4. Ellen G. White, *The Ministry of Healing* (Mountain View, CA: Pacific Press® Publishing Association, 1942), 143.

CHAPTER 1

Restoring the Image of God

Johnny Barnes: Reflecting God's image

Johnny Barnes was eighty-seven years old. He lived in Bermuda and wanted to do something for God. Johnny felt bad that he couldn't do much. He thought, *I have legs and arms that can walk and wave.* So Johnny picked a spot at a very busy intersection of his town where traffic often caused drivers to honk loudly and shout unkind words at each other. Every morning at five he would stand and wave his arms with welcoming joy and shout, "God loves you, and so do I! Have a wonderful day!" At first, people made fun of him. They thought he was just another crazy old man. At times they would throw things at him. But Johnny's presence was consistent. People got used to the contagious outpouring of love that they witnessed every morning.

One day, a couple of years later, drivers noticed that Johnny was not there. His presence was suddenly missed. Johnny's presence had become a symbol of friendly welcome in that part of town. Drivers contacted the local radio station to find out what had happened to him. Word went out that Johnny was sick and in the hospital; many people sent him flowers. Johnny's presence began to be equated with the friendliness that the community itself wanted to be known for.

In time, as a tribute to the influence and message of this persistently loving and joyful man, the government put a statue of Johnny Barnes at the intersection, with a welcoming smile and arms outstretched. Also a postage stamp was issued featuring Johnny.

The culture of that community was changed because of one man. In the place of angry shouting and the loud honking of car horns, there are kind words and friendly waves of hands. Today, those looking at Johnny's image in the form of a statue (and postage stamp) are reminded that this community in Bermuda values the legacy of a man who passionately demonstrated the love of God through his consistent presence.

Humankind and heavenly created beings— reflectors of God's image

The government officials intended that the statue should represent Johnny Barnes's expression of love and welcome. When we look at the Creation story in Genesis 1:26, we read, "Then God said, 'Let Us make man in Our image, according to Our likeness' " (NASB). God intended this image to represent the foundational nature of His kingdom, just as the image of Johnny Barnes reflects a message of welcome and love to all who visit his town in Bermuda.

God does not only have love, "God *is* love" (1 John 4:8, 16, NASB; emphasis added). This foundational truth is at the core of all Christian doctrine. Love represents the very nature of God. Love, by definition, is other-centered. God (love) is primarily represented as a triune Godhead, which for all of eternity models loving unity through an interactive relationship.

The love bond that holds the Godhead together for all of eternity led to the creation of heavenly beings that reflect the light of love and unity so characteristic of God. Each Member of the Godhead had a role in the creation of the heavenly host and planet Earth. God the Son (the Word) and God the Holy Spirit also joined God the Father in nurturing a government based on love and trust.

Because love does not exalt itself, the heavenly government did not emphasize hierarchy. The angel host was tasked with the responsibility of reflecting the love they receive and the brilliance of the character of their Creator.

The angel Lucifer, whose name means "bearer of light," served as a trusted agent among the angels to reflect God's character of love. Sadly, he chose to embark on a path of self-aggrandizement and self-centeredness. Instead of remaining under the lordship of his Creator—reflecting the light of God's love—Lucifer, the "light bearer," sought to be lord and create and bear his own light. He set in motion a rebellion that resulted in one-third of the angels defecting to a kingdom of darkness.

The Godhead had embarked on a plan to populate earth. They chose to bathe the planet in light and provide all the amenities needed for a healthy, heavenlike environment. The Godhead's crowning creation project was making "man" in Their image—male and female. They gave the male and female dominion over the entire creation (Genesis 1:26–28).

Adam and Eve were clothed in light and were to be stewards of a world that would represent the very essence of the character of the Creator. Love was woven into the very fabric of this new world, and Adam and Eve were to rule selflessly and lovingly and answer joyfully to God. As part of the creation of this planet, God set apart the seventh day of each week, on which Adam and Eve would celebrate God's finished work and nurture their love relationship with God and each other.

God's perfect creation in need of restoration

After Lucifer seduced Eve to sin and Eve tempted Adam into doing the same, God's perfect creation was terribly marred. It needed a thorough restoration. God's image was "well-nigh obliterated."[1] At their creation, our first parents had a likeness to their Creator physically, mentally, and spiritually (including socially).[2] To recover that image, a physical, mental, social, and spiritual restoration would be required; this will meet its ultimate fulfillment in the earth made new (Revelation 21:5).

It's interesting to note that the themes of Scripture have repeating patterns of *order, chaos,* and *restoration.*[3] One example is that in the beginning, God's creative work was what brought *order* to an earth that was "formless and empty" (Genesis 1:2). The Fall recorded in Genesis 3 was an example of *chaos,* and the promise of a Savior in Genesis 3:15 is an example of God's provision for *restoration.* Jesus, the promised Redeemer, demonstrated in His earthly ministry His goal of wholistically restoring humankind—physically, mentally, socially, and spiritually—through His healing miracles, His teaching, and His preaching. "It was His mission to bring to men *complete restoration;* He came to give them health and peace and perfection of character."[4]

Jesus' mission of restoration is the calling of His church. In numerous places in her writings, Ellen White frames this mission as "medical missionary work." For example, "Christ took a personal interest in men and women while He lived on this earth. He was a medical missionary everywhere He went. We are to go about doing good, even as He did. We are instructed to feed the hungry and clothe the naked, to heal the sick and comfort those that mourn."[5] The current label for "medical missionary work" is "comprehensive health ministry"—meaning completely restoring the whole person using the ministry method of Christ. In the chaos of this modern world, we are privileged to partner with Christ to bring wholistic restoration to the people in our communities.

There is a synergy between the physical, mental, social, and spiritual aspects of human beings. Each aspect affects the others. The following stories illustrate the wholistic ministry approach.

Adventist gospel work in Tanzania influences Maasai communities

Most Maasai communities have no keen interest in associating with other tribes because they are strict in observing their ancestral culture. Thus, it has been difficult to reach them with the gospel. However, God has opened ways of evangelizing the Maasai through various community services provided by Adventist churches in Tanzania that assist with physical, mental, social, and spiritual needs.

In the Southern Tanzania Union Mission, a physical need of Maasai communities was met by providing water in dry areas. The Misufini Seventh-day Adventist Church, Morogoro, drilled a borehole in a Maasai village known as Mkwajuni. Engineer Kisaka, a church member who works with the government, has initiated the digging of another borehole at Mbala, Chalinze, and the coast region. This community development project opened the hearts of the recipients to spiritual development. During a camp meeting, fifty Maasai people (the majority being male) gave their lives to Jesus.

In the Northern Tanzania Union Conference, the Karao Primary School was started by mobilizing Maasai children to attend kindergarten classes. With the influence of the primary school, Maasai parents, who formerly preferred marriage for their young girls instead of education, have requested that a girls' secondary school be built. Providing resources for mental development led to spiritual development; the Adventist Church membership in Karao amazingly increased from fifteen to seventy.

The impact of evangelism through education shows continued growth. Pastor and Mrs. Sungwon Cha, missionaries from South Korea, through their outreach activities in the remote areas of the North-East Tanzania Conference, started an adult English class for the Maasai at Lengijave, a village near the road from Arusha to Nairobi. English classes help with mental and social development as well as spiritual growth. This has made a big impact on the Maasai and helped them to love speaking English.

Many Maasai people have accepted Jesus Christ as their personal Savior through these physical, mental, social, and spiritual restoration activities, bringing a great awakening to Maasai communities in Tanzania.

Summersville Seventh-day Adventist Church: Restoring the image of God in its community

The Seventh-day Adventist church in Summersville, West Virginia, U.S.A., models wholistic ministry in the Appalachian area of the United States.

Wesley and Judy Olson and Jack and Marlys Jacobson planted this church in 1976. Later, a third couple, Steve and Donna Shank, joined them. Before coming to Summersville, all three couples had been medical missionaries—the Olsons and the Shanks in Guam and the Jacobsons in Okinawa. They wondered where and how God would use them when they returned to their homeland.

While in Guam, the Olsons saw a map in the *Adventist Review* that listed several "dark counties" where there were no Adventist congregations. This map inspired them to find a "dark county" where they could work when they returned to the United States. Their greatest wish was to bring their medical skills and the wholistic Adventist message to a place in the United States that needed them.

When the Olsons and Jacobsons returned to the United States, they began a six-week road trip across the country, starting in California and stopping at various places marked as possible locations to settle and do mission work. They drove all the way to Silver Spring, Maryland, and, so far, had no clear direction from God as to where they should serve.

There they met Thomas Mostert, the president of the Mountain View Conference in West Virginia, who said, "All I can offer you in West Virginia is a need." Pastor Mostert directed the Olsons and Jacobsons to look at Summersville.

After settling in the Summersville community, Jack and Wesley began working in the community's hospital. They started the hospital's night emergency room service. Soon they started something else: Bible studies with their new friends and coworkers.

In 1978, the two doctors opened a community medical clinic. The work of the clinic ended up being the entering wedge for the community to embrace future Adventist community services.

A year after the medical clinic opened, an Adventist school was launched because the Jacobsons and Olsons had six children between them. As of 2014, the school located on the church grounds has sixteen students—most of them from the community. Many of them need help with tuition costs through the worthy student fund the church operates. And there's more . . .

After the medical clinic was built, the lobby and later the basement were used as a place for weekly Sabbath worship, which provided a way to meet the spiritual needs of the church members serving the community, in addition to reaching those whom they served. As the group grew, they rented a local Methodist church while the Adventists, with the help of many volunteer laborers, built their own church.

The Jacobsons left Summersville around 1980. Soon Dr. Mark Wantz and his family joined the Summersville team, and two years later, Dr. Bruce and Sunita Greenburg came on board.

In 1986, the members of this little but growing church asked, "What else could our church do to contribute to this community?" Yes, they were already contributing to the community, but they wanted to meet more needs. As some of the members grappled with the idea of how to serve, God impressed them to start a child-care center. By talking to community leaders, that need was confirmed, since there was no child-care facility in the area. The Friends-R-Fun Child Development Center was started with eight children in the basement of the church, which doubled as a Sabbath School room. Through miracles God performed, a separate building was erected by mostly volunteer labor, including Maranatha.[6] Through the years, several additions have been added. The enrollment as of 2014 was 220 children, ranging in age from six weeks through twelve years. The center has always been state licensed, but now it is also nationally accredited. It is run by thirty full- and part-time staff, most of whom are not church members. The children's spiritual as well as mental, physical, and social needs are met with regular worship time, including songs and Bible stories.

In 1993, the Summersville Seventh-day Adventist Church took over a food pantry at the request of a Methodist minister who had started it in his own garage. Beginning with thirty-five families, today they provide food for around 350 family units.

Because more than one-third of the adults in the area didn't have a high school diploma, the church added an adult General Educational Development (GED) program in 1994. Now parents could study at the same place as their children in the family literacy program. Other classes were added so adults could benefit from parenting classes, nutrition and cooking classes, and so forth.

As the Summersville church members continued to bring wholistic restoration to people's lives, other community needs came to the church members' attention. For example, a big share of the population did not have health insurance and could not afford medical care. They did not qualify for government benefits or welfare, as they were the working poor. A federal grant was found that would address health needs in rural communities, and again the community leaders were called together for their input. The child-care center led the way in working together with the hospital, county board of education, and health department to write the grant and then to execute it when it was procured. The Summersville church's segment and the child-care center's segment were to provide community health education programs and to set up a free clinic for those who needed it. This free clinic is located on church property and continues to operate today.

At the same time, a need for an indoor physical education area (gymnasium) during inclement weather became apparent for the growing number of children at Friends-R-Fun and the Adventist school. It was decided early on that the gymnasium needed to be open for community groups to use as well as for the needs on campus. Money for the gym was raised, and a first-class gymnasium was built for the community to use and enjoy.

The objective of the Summersville church members is to connect with their community and to respond as they discover needs. They offer further resources, such as programs for smoking cessation, overcoming depression, and so on.

The Summersville church members meet the community's spiritual needs by doing one-on-one Bible studies with people, taking to heart Sider, Olson, and Unruh's advice that "the core feature of a holistic approach to social ministry is finding ways of sharing the Good News of salvation with those you serve. Holistic ministry treats each individual as a precious, unique, complex creation stamped with the image of God."[7]

As of 2014, the Summersville Seventh-day Adventist Church has one hundred members with an average attendance of about sixty. The church is relatively small for all the various services and community outreach projects it has. The only way those services can be accomplished is by working alongside community members to provide the services. Community service and witnessing are not only for those we serve, but also for those we serve *with*.

The members of God's church are made in God's image. Love is the main attribute of that image. This love will drive us to realize that *all* the people in our communities are also made in God's image. He calls us to work with Him in restoring them physically, mentally, socially, and spiritually—as demonstrated by the Summersville Seventh-day Adventist Church.[8]

Start thinking about expanding your church's ministry for the people in its neighborhood to be wholistic: *physical, mental, social,* and *spiritual* restoration. Subsequent chapters in this book will better explain how to do this.

1. Ellen G. White, *Education* (Mountain View, CA: Pacific Press® Publishing Association, 1952), 15.

2. Ibid.

3. We are indebted to Tiago Costa Arrais for this concept.

4. White, *The Ministry of Healing,* 17; emphasis added.

5. Ellen G. White, *Welfare Ministry* (Washington, DC: Review and Herald® Publishing Association, 1952), 328.

6. Maranatha Volunteers International is a supporting ministry of the Seventh-day Adventist Church. Maranatha's mission is to organize volunteers to build urgently needed buildings throughout the world.

7. Sider, Olson, and Unruh, *Churches That Make a Difference*, 90.

8. For more information on the story of the Summersville Seventh-day Adventist Church, see Jean Kellner, "From Acorn to Oak Tree," *Adventist Review*, July 19, 2007, accessed September 24, 2015, http://archives.adventistreview.org/article/1263/archives/issue-2007-1520/from-acorn-to-oak-tree.

CHAPTER 2

Restoring Dominion

Restoring God's image restores dominion

The church had twenty-four members when it started; four years later, it had 155 members. A group of social workers were the catalyst for starting this congregation in Delft, Netherlands. The social workers had established Alivio, a foundation connected with the church that assists teen mothers in the community. The young mothers are loved and accepted but are also taught to accept responsibility for their decisions. Alivio gives them tools to deal with their circumstances. Many of these young women ask for prayer and now attend church. The Alivio Foundation has expanded its support to include counseling for local young men, for "they also need to be taught responsibility for their actions," one participant commented. "As the Alivio Foundation expands, staff members hope to open a shelter to 'guide and counsel' women in need and offer them mental, spiritual, social and financial rehabilitation."[1]

The Delft church is cooperating with God to move these women toward experiencing God's image being restored in them—physically, mentally, socially, and spiritually. Also, the church is helping them with the next step: taking responsibility for their actions, their lives, and their environment.

This follows the creation model: before humans could have dominion (stewardship) of the earth, they had to reflect God's image: "Then God said, 'Let Us make man in Our image, according to Our likeness;

19

let them have dominion over the fish of the sea, over the birds of the air, and over the cattle, over all the earth and over every creeping thing that creeps on the earth' " (Genesis 1:26, NKJV). After being made in God's image, Adam and Eve had dominion (stewardship) over the earth, under God's dominion over them (verses 27, 28). The same is true today: before we can effectively have dominion over our environment and our own lives, we must be whole. "It means that in the whole being—the body, the mind, as well as the soul—the image of God is to be restored."[2] The ultimate step of being restored in God's image happens in this way: "As the perfection of His character is dwelt upon, the mind is renewed, and the soul is re-created in the image of God."[3]

The book *Education* also links wholistic restoration with humankind realizing their "divine purpose": "To restore in man the image of his Maker, to bring him back to the perfection in which he was created, to promote the development of body, mind, and soul, *that the divine purpose in his creation might be realized*—this was to be the work of redemption."[4]

Dominion—the divine purpose of humankind's creation

When God created humankind in His image to rule "over all the earth" (verse 26, NKJV), the list of examples given did not mention everything over which they ruled or had stewardship. For example, plants and trees were not mentioned, but Genesis 2:15 says, "The LORD God took the man and put him in the Garden of Eden to work it and take care of it." However, the phrase "over all the earth" covers every living thing on the earth.

Psalm 8 emphasizes the kingly rulership part of humankind's raison d'être with the concept that God made humankind "a little lower than the heavenly beings and *crowned* [us] with glory and honor" so we could rule over the works of God's hands; everything was put under humanity's feet (verses 5, 6, ESV; emphasis added). However, in filling this glorious role, we must factor in Isaiah 43:7, which adds another shade of meaning to the purpose for which humankind was created: we are created for *His* glory.

Ecology and ruling over the works of God's hands

In the biblical stewardship model, we see that God Himself loves and cares for His creation (Isaiah 40:12). God provides for land and sea animals, birds, and even for the land itself (Job 38:26, 27; Psalm 104:10–12, 14, 25, 27, 28). If God is so careful to provide for His creatures, it is clear that an important part of our job description is to lovingly care for them and their environment—the earth and the sea. However, in doing this, we must focus on worshiping the Creator rather than created things (Romans 1:25).

One Adventist church plant in Carnegie, Pennsylvania, partnered with a local nature organization and beautified their community by planting trees. In addition to beautifying their communities, churches and members can model and promote stewardship of the earth by recycling; using less paper; using less energy (consider conducting an energy audit in your church); promoting vegetarianism; properly disposing of litter; walking and biking more, and driving less; holding a Creation Sabbath worship service; organizing a Creation Celebration event for the community to enjoy the outdoors with your congregation; holding Bible studies on the environment; adopting a local park, river, or roadway for cleaning and restoration, if needed; organizing a church or community garden; and so forth.[5]

"Under his feet" and victory over the enemy

In Psalm 8:6, we read, "You make him to rule over the works of Your hands; You have put all things *under his feet*" (NASB; emphasis added).[6] The phrase "under his feet" also has the connotation of victory over an enemy.[7] The "enemy" could be anything in our lives—addiction, poverty, unemployment, a broken relationship—that tries to enslave us and block us from being good stewards over that which God has given us dominion. This dominion includes our personal lives as well as the care of the earth.

Galatians 5:23 lists "self-control" as part of the fruit of the Spirit (NASB). This "self-control" is *enkráteia,* taking its sense "from the stem *krat*—denoting power or lordship." *Enkráteia* means "dominion over the self or something."[8] Clearly, this dominion must be guided by the indwelling Holy Spirit.

Hebrews 2:6–18 extends the meaning of "everything" or "all things" in Psalm 8:6 so as to show that once again, through the victory of Jesus Christ over Satan, humankind will regain the dominion it has lost. In the *Seventh-day Adventist Bible Commentary,* in the comments on Psalm 8:6, we read, "Through Christ man is capable of mastery over himself, over the lower orders of creation, and over his fellows, in mutual subjection to the dominion of Christ."[9] Note that though humankind is capable of mastery over our "fellows," when we are under the dominion of Christ, we will not *dominate* our "fellows."

Limitations to and conditions of humanity's dominion

Our first parents did *not* have rulership, or dominion, over the "tree of the knowledge of good and evil" (Genesis 2:17, NASB). They were to have nothing to do with it! And they were not to have dominion over each other, in the sense of being dominating or controlling.

We cannot lose track of the fact that Adam and Eve were subject to God's dominion over them. They were responsible to God's sovereign rule over them to the same degree that all of nature was subject to them.

The role of the church in restoring dominion in people's lives

In *Churches That Make a Difference,* Sider, Olson, and Unruh have explained how a church can be used by God to help people in its community better manage, or restore, dominion in their chaotic lives.[10] When a church plans its outreach in a community, it's important to consider the types of social ministries the church will use to accomplish this. Sider, Olson, and Unruh state that social ministries fall into four basic categories:

1. Relief
2. Individual development
3. Community development
4. Structural change (advocacy)

Relief includes directly providing clothing, food, or shelter to people who are in urgent need. Relief is like giving hungry people fish. Most churches operate at the relief level.

Individual development involves ministries that are personal and transformational, enabling people to improve their physical, intellectual, emotional, relational, or social status. *Individual development is like teaching people how to fish.*

For example, this means providing education to improve job skills, parenting skills, health, and so on. It could mean mentoring that empowers individuals to help themselves.

Community development helps to reconstruct the elements of a healthy community, such as renewing housing, providing jobs, and improving education and health care. *Community development is like providing fishing tools.* Sometimes people can experience individual development, but the environment of their community is unhealthy and continues to drag them down, even though they have been developed individually. Community development seeks to improve the services and environment of a whole community, such as by providing affordable housing, health-care facilities or services, and educational facilities or services. "Development that does not promote the welfare of the whole community has missed the mark."[11]

Structural change means the transformation of unfair, unjust economic, environmental, political, or cultural systems or institutions. *Structural change is like making sure everyone in the community has equal access to the fishing pond.*

At times, it is obvious that there are unjust practices in a community, such as racial or economic discrimination, corruption in local government or industries, or disregard for safety issues. Sometimes the church may have to go to the top of various levels of government or industry to speak for those who have no voice, to promote justice, to highlight the changes that are needed to help the people affected, and to improve their lives and community.

Coatesville, Pennsylvania, Seventh-day Adventist Church pursuing the four types of social ministry

In the winter of 1983, W. W. Fordham, pastor of the First Seventh-day Adventist Church of Coatesville, Pennsylvania, U.S.A., told his small church that he didn't want to be the pastor of a church whose doors were locked throughout the week except Wednesday nights and Sabbaths. He stated that the church is the best real estate in any community and should be open throughout the week to serve the community. Because, at this point, no one in the church knew what effectively serving the community should look like, the members realized they must go to the community and ask.

After developing a prayer team to guide the church according to God's will, a church assessment was completed, noting the interests and spiritual gifts of church members. Second, church members went in teams to ask the community about its needs, interests, and assets. Finally, a small committee was formed to assess the services of community providers. Members of this committee asked providers what service they provided and what remained in the category of unmet needs. The latter inquiry provided the church's niche list.

The most valuable information came from city officials, local police officers, and the county Department of Community Development. Church members were surprised to learn that their city needed shelter for homeless men, women, and families. This illustrates the need to ask the community what its needs are (and not to guess), as the homeless were invisible to members in their city. No one knew this was a problem in the county; after all, it ranked as the twenty-sixth most affluent county in North America.

To the credit of the Coatesville church leadership, within three weeks a twenty-five-bed-capacity shelter opened for men, women, children, and displaced youth in the church building. Cots were set up in the open meeting area for men, and families were placed in Sabbath School rooms. The church provided the residents with basic necessities and an address and telephone number. They changed the church's usual greeting on the answering machine so people calling in wouldn't know it was a shelter: "Hello, we're not available. Please leave a message." People had no idea they had just called a church. Residents would receive messages; for example, "Jim, you have a job interview on Tuesday."

This shelter in the church is an example of the *relief* type of social ministry. Shelter volunteers observed a phenomenal trend. Men, especially, moved toward self-sufficiency with just their basic needs being met. This was an unexpected scenario. Having eliminated the concern about where they would sleep or find food, they could then focus on employment, benefits they may have been entitled to, and family.

In September 1988, the Allegheny East Conference of Seventh-day Adventists loaned money to the Coatesville church to purchase a hospital building in Coatesville that had been empty for thirteen years.[12] The purchased hospital was renamed the W. C. Atkinson Memorial Community Services Center—in honor of Dr. Whittier C. Atkinson, an African American physician who built the first portion of the hospital in 1936.

In January 1992, having sheltered men, women, families, and

occasionally runaway or "throwaway" youth in the church for six years, the shelter relocated to the newly renovated former hospital, where a twenty-two-bed shelter was developed for homeless men. Nearly two hundred men shelter there annually. "We have an open-door policy, just like the heart of God," said Minnie McNeil, the Allegheny East Conference Adventist Community Services Center director and former chair of the nonprofit that runs the Atkinson center. Meanwhile, a shelter for single women and women with children was established in the city by another organization, removing the need to provide shelter for women and children at the Atkinson center.

The renovated hospital provided significant space for the development of additional services that the local church leadership discovered were needed. This would fulfill the church's goal of not only caring for God's people as good stewards, but also restoring broken people to a point where they are able to be good stewards themselves.

The Atkinson complex provided space for many kinds of *individual development* opportunities, for individual development is about change and not just charity. First of all, the homeless shelter produced stability for its guests. The Atkinson staff provided case management, mentoring, modeling, and support as well as instruction in job readiness and preparedness and the opportunity to complete a GED for guests who had not completed high school. Through the years, ongoing community assessment has generated a plethora of community programs and services at Atkinson to empower guests in the shelter and community people in their personal lives: regular Alcoholics Anonymous and Narcotics Anonymous meetings, diabetes support groups, grandparent support groups, computer literacy classes, English as a second language classes, piano and organ lessons with an annual recital, youth summer camp, community gardening, creative arts and photography instruction, afterschool homework assistance, weekly health seminars, spiritual enrichment, and many more.

Eventually, in addition to the men's shelter, two transitional houses adjacent to the Atkinson center were procured and renovated. Men from the shelter who are moving toward self-sufficiency yet still need additional support are invited to relocate to the transitional homes. The men work, pay rent, and volunteer in the community—another stage of their individual development.

Community development occurred from the time the original homeless shelter opened at the Coatesville church through the improvement of the environment. The transitional houses are examples of community development, as are eighteen apartments in the Atkinson center that are rented by persons in the community with low to moderate income. Other community developments were ignited by the Atkinson center's presence in the community, such as neighborhood safety, beautification, and rehabilitation projects. This produced community pride.

The Atkinson center offered a health center for twelve years to help build up the community's resources and promote community health. Local physicians volunteered their time to staff the center. Health education on the eight natural remedies was included with the health center's services.[13] Years later, a second health center was opened in the community by another organization, so the Atkinson clients were transferred.

Structural change is also part of the Atkinson center's mission; and through the years, it has advocated for important community issues, including employment, health care, honorable care of veterans, and affordable housing.

Through advocacy for structural change, three dilapidated townhouses were transformed from crack houses into new housing opportunities. The Atkinson center negotiated with local, county, and federal leaders (Department of Housing and Urban Development) and acquired these houses. The federal government agreed to rebuild the old houses, and the city built new sidewalks. Additionally, the government continues to own and maintain the beautiful, newly rebuilt homes. There are eight units—with an additional unit for the facility manager—providing permanent housing for several formerly homeless men who pay their own rent. The tenants in these homes are disabled but have steady jobs or are on permanent disability grants.

The influence of the Atkinson center has provided an impetus for community-wide revitalization, not only in the Coatesville environment but in the lives of the people they have served. For example, one of the first permanent housing residents, who had previously been in the shelter for three years, found Jesus while at the Atkinson center and was baptized. He became the first facility manager and was reunited with his wife after fifteen years of separation. His wife is taking Bible studies from the Coatesville church pastor (the vice president of the Atkinson center), and they are preparing for their heavenly home. "We continue reaping the rewards of seeing lives transformed," says Minnie McNeil.

> Start thinking of ways to expand your church's ministry for the people in its neighborhood to include the four types of social ministry: *relief, individual development, community development,* and *structural change.* Give ideas for each one.

---

1. Rajmund Dabrowski and Adventist News Network, "Antillean Adventists in Delft Assist Teenage Mothers," Adventist New Network bulletin, March 11, 2010, http://news.adventist.org/all-news/news/go/2010-03-11/antillean-adventists-in-delft-assist-teenage-mothers/.

2. Ellen G. White, *Education,* 16.

3. Ibid., 18.

4. Ibid., 15, 16; emphasis supplied. To dig deeper into comments on the created-in-God's-image-for-dominion or rulership model (Genesis 1:26–28), read all of chapter 1 in *Education.*

5. This ideas list is adapted from *The Green Bible* (New York: HarperCollins Publishers, 2008). For other ideas on stewardship of the earth, go to http://creationcare.org/.

6. The King James Version renders Psalm 8:6 as "Thou madest him to have dominion over the works of thy hands; thou hast put all things under his feet."

7. See, e.g., Matthew 22:44; Psalm 110:1; 1 Kings 5:3; Acts 2:34, 35; 1 Corinthians 15:25; Hebrews 1:13; 10:13.

8. See Geoffrey W. Bromiley, *Theological Dictionary of the New Testament,* eds. Gerhard Kittel and Gerhard Friedrich (Grand Rapids, MI: Eerdmans, 1985), s.v. *"enkráteia."*

9. *The Seventh-day Adventist Bible Commentary,* ed. F. D. Nichol (Hagerstown, MD: Review and Herald®, 1977), 3:649.

10. See Sider, Olson, and Unruh, *Churches That Make a Difference.*

11. Harvie M. Conn and Manuel Ortiz, *Urban Ministry: The Kingdom, the City & the People of God* (Downers Grove, IL: InterVarsity Press, 2001), 357.

12. Twenty-five years later, in 2013, the members of the nonprofit arm of the First Seventh-day Adventist Church of Coatesville gained full ownership of the complex when the $1.5 million in renovations were finally paid in full.

13. "Pure air, sunlight, abstemiousness, rest, exercise, proper diet, the use of water, trust in divine power—these are the true remedies." White, *The Ministry of Healing,* 127.

Social Justice in the Old Testament—Part 1

A compelling call to action

Metri Manohar could not forget the sight on that particular afternoon: it was raining heavily; the wind was blowing hard; and the weather was cold. As an Adventist literature evangelist from Andhra Pradesh in India, he was on his way to a hotel on August 22, 1999, to have lunch with some publishing department directors. While he and his colleagues took shelter under a roof, he saw a young woman about eighteen to twenty years old who lacked proper clothing—she wore only a towel around her waist and a half-torn top. Her hair was unkempt, and she stank.

In the heavy rain she was collecting plastic "papers" from the trash bin. Brother Manohar watched her carefully as she took those papers and moved to a nearby concrete beam. He was shocked to see a small baby lying there on the ground, completely drenched in rainwater. This mother, who was mentally ill, went to her baby and took it to her bosom with love and compassion. She started to cover her baby to keep it warm, wrapping the baby with the papers from the tip of the toes to the neck to protect the little one from the cold climate. What a great demonstration of motherly love!

Brother Manohar was very touched and sad to see such a situation, and his heart was moved with pity. He said to one of his colleagues, "Sir, something is going on. Have a glance." Brother Manohar's colleague observed for a few minutes, and then he said, "Manohar, there are so many people like this. We can't do anything." He tapped Brother Manohar's shoulder and made him leave the scene. The men moved forward, but Brother Manohar's eyes and concentration were on that pitiful young woman and her sufferings. Just as God did during the time of Israel's slavery to Egypt, Brother Manohar heard and saw her groan of suffering (see Exodus 2:23–25). That evening he shared this incident with his wife, and she was also touched by the infirmities of people around her.

Months passed by; Brother Manohar could not find peace and started questioning himself: If the same situation happened in his family, would he keep quiet about it? Would it not bother him?

Then an idea struck him: he could be the answer. He thought, *Why should I not do something to eradicate the pain in situations like this?* He actively started searching for ways in which he could help such people. With all his heart, he was willing to serve "the least of these" (Matthew 25:40). But he didn't know how to effectively reach out to help them. To learn, Brother Manohar had long conversations regarding this issue with many people—religious leaders, politicians, elderly people. They said, "It is not an easy job to take care of such people. It is highly risky. It is a life-and-death matter." After all these conversations, he decided to do or die.

His resolve led him to take a law course to study the issue. He diligently studied about mental illness and the destitute and did research on mentally ill people. In his studies, Brother Manohar searched for answers to his questions: What are the factors that lead to mental illness? What are the reasons behind it? While studying, Brother Manohar continued doing literature evangelist work so that he and his family could survive.

After a long period of research, he started an Adventist nongovernmental organization to benefit the mentally ill and destitute of society—those who are roaming on the roads without food, clothes, and shelter. As of 2013, more than six hundred men and women, rendered destitute in the course of their battle against mental illness and found wandering in the streets of the Hyderabad area of India, have been sheltered at Brother Manohar's residential care and transit home. Of these, more than 270 men and women have been reunited with their families after a period of sustained care, treatment, and psychological help. Many have accepted Jesus Christ as their personal Savior.

There were two different reactions to the scene of a destitute mother and baby on that day in August 1999: Brother Manohar responded with action, while his colleague responded with indifference. "The righteous care about justice for the poor, but the wicked have no such concern" (Proverbs 29:7). How do you measure up in relation to this passage of Scripture? Metri Manohar and his team have powerfully demonstrated the love of a compassionate God with their efforts to make a difference by bringing social justice to the Hyderabad community in Jesus' name.

God's call to be a prophetic voice

In the Hebrew Scriptures, we find that the call for social justice requires a prophetic voice, which calls God's people to intentionality. Walter Harrelson summarizes four elements of prophetic teaching:

1. Some prophetic messages are warnings that are always a matter of life and death, calling for the rejection of evil and for making a commitment to God (Deuteronomy 30:15–20).
2. God cares for those who are without protection in society, such as widows, orphans, slaves, debtors, strangers, and the homeless (Exodus 23:3; Deuteronomy 16:19, 20). His prophetic voice prohibits unjust differences or partiality on our part, and hoarding property and excluding the privilege of a hurting community (Isaiah 5:8).
3. God calls for obedience and justice over formal worship and sacrifice. Ethical behavior must spring from right motives—loving as God loves (Deuteronomy 7:6–11; see also Amos 5:21–24; 8:4–6).
4. God motivates His prophets to present a message that is contemporary and full of hope in the light of eschatology and the apocalypse, focused not only on the day-to-day struggle of survival, but on the final affirmation that God will succeed in His plan for His creation and win the battle between good and evil, bringing salvation to His people, spiritually and tangibly.[1]

Which aspect of the prophetic role have Seventh-day Adventists usually emphasized? Zdravko Plantak comments that Adventism tends to emphasize the fourth aspect of the prophetic role—a preoccupation with making predictions and interpreting prophecy—especially in an evangelistic and theological sense.[2] Additionally, God calls His church to actively participate in His mission to transform the world and act as a channel flowing with abundant life in Jesus *now* (John 10:10)! God wants us to bring the kingdom of heaven—a foretaste of heaven—to our communities *now,* prophetically pointing people to the assurance, not only the hope, of a kingdom of glory to come (Matthew 6:10).

Plantak challenges Adventists to be faithful to their prophetic calling by considering other aspects of prophetic ministry. A primary focus is the socio-ethical role of prophets. The theme of social concern appears in most of the Old Testament Major and Minor Prophets.[3] In 1914, Ellen White gave an emphatic admonition to Adventist Church members: "Many deplore the wrongs which they know exist, but consider themselves free from all responsibility in the matter. This cannot be. Every individual exerts an influence in society."[4]

God's rebuke and plea to His unjust covenant people

God Himself is the Author and Model of justice. The psalmist proclaims, "I know that the LORD secures justice for the poor and upholds the cause of the needy" (Psalm 140:12). There is reason to believe that, at least for the Old Testament, the two words *mishpat* ("justice") and *tsdaqa* ("righteousness") can be used interchangeably. This begs the question: Are we only focused on being right? Are we giving equal emphasis to being just and nurturing justice in our community?

Throughout Scripture, we find descriptions of the behavior of those who are called just, or righteous. The Bible shows that the difference between the righteous and the wicked is often measured by their treatment of the underdog. The Old Testament is replete with warnings and admonitions to God's covenant people—His "true church" in that era. His chosen people and their leaders had a basic knowledge of the Hebrew Scriptures, professed to follow Him, and had a form of godliness. But this was not enough. For example, the prophet Isaiah writes that their profession and form were so hypocritical and far from the ways of God that God equated and identified them with the people of Sodom and Gomorrah (Isaiah 1:10–17).

God's call to cure spiritual laryngitis

Again and again God has called His people to be cured of spiritual "laryngitis" and to "speak up for those who cannot speak for themselves, for the rights of all who are destitute," to "judge fairly," and to "defend the rights of the poor and needy" (Proverbs 31:8, 9). This could mean the church confronting unjust governments and organizations to defend the defenseless or actively confronting disturbing social issues.

An example of responding to God's call to "speak up for those who cannot speak for themselves" is enditnow, a campaign launched in 2009 by the Seventh-day Adventist Church to stop violence against women. This campaign—a partnership between the Adventist Development and Relief Agency and the Department of Women's Ministries of the Seventh-day Adventist Church—has extended to more than two hundred countries. It aims to mobilize Adventists around the world and invite other community groups to join in to resolve this serious worldwide issue. Online resources to create awareness and share solutions are available for each person in this global movement. Global activities include enditnow rallies, educational activities, advocacy, petitions, speeches, art displays, financial support, and so forth.[5] In addition to enditnow, the Adventist Church holds an Abuse Prevention Emphasis Day, which is typically held the fourth Saturday of every August.

God has something to say about activities such as this: "I'm GOD, and I act in loyal love. I do what's right and set things right and fair, and delight in those who do the same things" (Jeremiah 9:24, *The Message*).

God's call to end self-centered religion

An examination of Isaiah 58 reveals that God has no use for individuals who perceive their religious duty as a chore to be endured to arrest the attention of God. God's anger is directed at people who fast religiously but only think of their own hunger (verse 3). Such fasting often ends in seeking to manipulate others and criticizing those who do not conform to their self-made rules. This leads to a self-centered religion that does not serve God.

God's solution pushes us beyond self-centeredness to a fast that simply places the needs of others as higher priorities than our own needs (verses 6–10). The rest of Isaiah 58 challenges every generation of believers to view themselves as products of God's workmanship and find joy in the Lord who is Creator, Redeemer, Guide, and Satisfier of our every need (verse 11). The result is that

> "your people will rebuild the ancient ruins
>   and will raise up the age-old foundations;
> you will be called Repairer of Broken Walls,
>   Restorer of Streets with Dwellings" (verse 12).

The "Streets with Dwellings" are communities, neighborhoods.

God's Sabbath as a call to social justice

Sabbath attitude. The pattern of Isaiah 58 illustrates and indicates a Sabbath attitude (verses 13, 14) that celebrates the other-centeredness that comes when we all (rich and poor alike) realize it's not what we do or have done, but rather what God has done and is doing when we labor in His strength and enter into His rest.[6]

Sabbath—an equalizer. The jubilee sabbath—one of the three biblical sabbaths—was an equalizer of people by leveling the playing field (Leviticus 25:8–55). Likewise, the seventh-day Sabbath helps us to realize that religion is less about us and all about our acknowledgment of our dependence on God. Ronald J. Sider admonishes that "if Christians could recover the practice of the Sabbath, it would help us turn away from the mad consumerism that is destroying people and the environment. . . . And in those quiet times in the divine presence, the God of the poor would transform our materialistic hearts and make us more generous."[7]

Avoiding buying and selling on the Sabbath is an equalizer of the haves and have-nots—at least for one day a week. It's a weekly reminder of God's desire for equality in our society at all times.

Sabbath as resistance. Not only is the Sabbath an equalizer; it is a form of resisting service to the "other gods" (Exodus 20:3) of insatiable productivity and "not enough" that keep people in a state of hopeless weariness. Instead of a constant pressure to produce, the Sabbath offers a time to focus on resting in the finished work of God.

The Sabbath becomes resistance to anxiety. When we choose not to oppress others and ourselves with a restless anxiety that has no limit or termination, we break the anxiety cycle. We serve the all-powerful God of the universe, who rests on the Sabbath and graciously invites all His people to join Him—rich, middle class, and poor.

The Sabbath calls for resistance to coercion by reminding God's people that they were created to rule over what God has entrusted to them (Genesis 1:26–28), instead of being ruled by someone or something else. Stopping work for the Sabbath was unheard of for a slave, and it demonstrates resistance to being subjected to coercion by someone else. Also, the Sabbath resists coercion by society, which forces everyone to perform better, produce more, and consume more. Such coercion creates the "haves" and the "have-nots." Sabbath observance demonstrates that *all* classes "may rest, as you do" (Deuteronomy 5:14). All have equal worth, value, and rest.[8]

The Sabbath becomes resistance to exclusivism because, under God's government, there is an invitation for all to come into God's kingdom. No one is excluded from the kingdom if they choose to claim God as their King. Isaiah 56 makes the Sabbath a single specific requirement for membership in God's kingdom. Sabbath keeping indicates that anyone who truly observes it is defined by justice, compassion, and mercy, and not competition, achievement, production, or acquisition.

The Sabbath offers resistance to multitasking by providing a magnetic focus on God. This focus prevents the double-mindedness exhibited by those who claim to be worshiping while allowing their minds to be buying and selling and indulging in self-serving at the expense of the poor (Isaiah 58; Amos 8:4–6).[9]

And finally, the Sabbath is designed to free us from a coveting mindset. "Coveting . . . consists in the pursuit of commodity at the expense of the neighbor. Sabbath is a big no for both; it is no to the worship of commodity; it is no to the pursuit of commodity. But it is more than no. Sabbath is the regular, disciplined, visible, concrete yes to the neighborly reality of the community beloved by God."[10]

A social justice benediction

In response to the calls of the prophets, reflect on the following:

> May God bless you with *discomfort* at easy answers, half-truths, and superficial relationships, so that you may live deep within your heart.
> May God bless you with *anger* at injustice, oppression, and

exploitation of people, so that you may work for justice, freedom, and peace.

May God bless you with *tears* to shed for those who suffer from pain, rejection, starvation, and war, so that you may reach out your hand to comfort them and to turn their pain into joy.

And may God bless you with enough *foolishness* to believe that you can make a difference in this world, so that you can do what others claim cannot be done.[11]

Amen.

Look around you. Find a situation of extreme need that seems beyond your ability to help, and do something *that you can* to help.

1. Walter Harrelson, "Prophetic Ethics," in *A New Dictionary of Christian Ethics,* eds. John Macquarrie and James F. Childress (London: SCM Press, 1986), 508–512.

2. See Zdravko Plantak, "A Prophetic Community Today: Imaginary Visionaries and Social Actionaries for the Third Millennium," in *Exploring the Frontiers of Faith: Festschrift in Honour of Dr. Jan Paulsen,* Congratulatory ed., eds. Børge Schantz and Reinder Bruinsma (Lüneburg: Advent-Verlag, 2009), 139–155.

3. Ibid.

4. Ellen G. White, "The Temperance Cause," *Advent Review and Sabbath Herald,* October 15, 1914, 1.

5. Information retrieved from http://www.enditnow.org/.

6. This Sabbath attitude is illustrated in the three types of biblical sabbaths, where social justice is highlighted in a setting of a relationship with God: (1) the weekly Sabbaths (Exodus 20; Leviticus 23; Deuteronomy 5; Isaiah 58); (2) the sabbaths of years (Exodus 23:9–12; Leviticus 25; Deuteronomy 15); (3) the year of jubilee: after seven sabbaths of years was the year of jubilee (Leviticus25).

7. Ronald J. Sider, *Rich Christians in an Age of Hunger: Moving From Affluence to Generosity* (Nashville, TN: Thomas Nelson, 2005), 207, quoted in Dwight K. Nelson, *Pursuing the Passion of Jesus* (Nampa, ID: Pacific Press® Publishing Association, 2005), 86.

8. Richard Rice suggests that every practice that deprives human beings of their sense of dignity and worth contradicts the message of the Sabbath. See Richard Rice, *The Reign of God: An Introduction to Christian Theology From a Seventh-day Adventist Perspective* (Berrien Springs, MI: Andrews University Press, 1997), 320.

9. This section on Sabbath as resistance is adapted from Walter Brueggemann, *Sabbath as Resistance: Saying No to the Culture of Now* (Louisville, KY: Westminster John Knox Press, 2014).

10. Ibid., 86, 87.

11. Quoted in Eldin Villafañe, *Beyond Cheap Grace: A Call to Radical Discipleship, Incarnation, and Justice* (Grand Rapids, MI: Eerdmans, 2006), 81. This prayer is often attributed to Saint Francis of Assisi.

Social Justice in the Old Testament—Part 2

Casa Amar—bringing new life to the desperate homeless

Life as a migrant is difficult. But life as a migrant without a home, job, and the basic necessities of life is even worse. *Casa Amar,* "House of Love," is a place of refuge for homeless and destitute people in Nuevo Laredo, a port city at the northern tip of the Mexican state of Tamaulipas. Across the Rio Grande from Laredo, Texas, U.S.A., Nuevo Laredo was formerly part of the original settlement of Laredo, which is now in Texas. In 1848, after the Mexican-American War, Nuevo Laredo broke off of Laredo and became part of Mexico. In this border city, where drug cartels have turf wars as they compete for control of the drug trade into the United States, Casa Amar is a loving home, providing emergency shelter and protection for migrants from Honduras, El Salvador, Guatemala, Mexico, and other countries.

Pastor Ervin Ortiz and his church in Laredo, Texas, have reached "across the border" to help Nuevo Laredo resident and Adventist church member Aaron Mendez fulfill his dream of starting and maintaining a shelter for the migrants of Nuevo Laredo. At first, Aaron received four people. At the time of this writing, he and his staff serve eighty. At first, Aaron worked at his regular job in the morning but spent his afternoons taking care of these desperate people. After six months, Aaron decided to dedicate himself full time at the Casa Amar Migrant Center. He depends on personal donations to sustain this vital ministry.

Aaron sees Casa Amar as a place to supply physical, mental, social, and spiritual needs. Not only does he endeavor to provide a temporary home for his guests on earth, but he is providing opportunities for them to prepare for their eternal heavenly home.

The daily program at Casa Amar is structured. At 6:00 A.M., the guests wake up. A worship service follows at 6:30, with breakfast at 7:00. After breakfast, everyone is required to leave the shelter and do something. Generally, the "something" is looking for a job. The guests are not permitted to use alcohol, illegal drugs, or tobacco inside Casa Amar, or anywhere else while they are guests there; the goal is to move them toward a healthier and more responsible lifestyle. The guests all take part in maintaining Casa Amar as they help in preparing food, serving, and cleaning.

At 4:00 P.M., Casa Amar opens again to receive guests as they return from work. Vespers is at 6:30 P.M. Generally, a guest speaker presents biblical teachings; and the guests pray, learn the Ten Commandments, and read the Bible together. By God's grace, many lives are being changed from these spiritual disciplines. Those who live at Casa Amar or visit there say it is a place where you can feel the presence of the Lord.

The guests know that Saturday is the Lord's Day. In the beginning of Casa Amar's existence, the migrants were all taken to a local Seventh-day Adventist church each Sabbath. As the number of guests has increased, Casa Amar has become another church by itself. Every three months there is a baptism. Most of the migrants make their decisions to make Christ the Lord of their lives and to be baptized after a week of evangelistic reaping meetings.

At the time of this writing, Casa Amar has been open for four years. Its eighty guests receive two meals a day, clothing, and a place to sleep. Families, women, men, and minors are all welcome; once a baby was born there. The guests can stay as long as they need to, but the average is one month.

After two years, Casa Amar was registered as a nonprofit organization. The local government has recognized Cara Amar's good work and helps financially, as do other organizations and local stores. Currently, Casa Amar is renting a building; however, there are plans to buy land and build a facility when the needed hundred thousand dollars is raised.

Casa Amar has made a profound impact in its city; through its efforts, many lives have been transformed. It is a place of hope, where migrants find their best Friend, Jesus. Many people are now serving Jesus because Casa Amar served them in His name in their time of great need.

These migrants of Nuevo Laredo, Mexico, were disconnected, powerless, homeless, and hopeless, just like the Israelite captives in Babylon who were disconnected from and deprived of their homes. Ezekiel 37 describes the captives as dry and dead bones with no apparent hope of life. God brought them back to life, and they were revived for a mission! Fast-forward to Ezekiel 47. These dead, dry, and seemingly hopeless "house of Israel" bones have changed from dead to life giving. Read on for the rest of the story.

Bringing life to a dead valley

Two groups had been wrenched out of Jerusalem. While Daniel and his friends were sent to Babylon, a large population of Judean citizens was sent to work on a canal off the Euphrates River, to the southeast of Babylon. These captives had lost their land, their capital city, their king, the temple of God, and their identity as a people. Hopelessness often engulfed them as they considered that, as a nation, they were dead. God heard their pleas for an answer to their despair and sent the prophet Ezekiel to bring hope to the captives in the canal trenches where the majority worked. Among the messages directed to the captives is the vision of the dry bones found in Ezekiel 37.

After having been placed in the middle of a valley full of dry, scattered bones, Ezekiel was asked one question and given one command. The question was simple, though hard to answer: "Son of man, can these bones live?" (Ezekiel 37:3). Possibly not wanting to implicate himself, Ezekiel wisely chose to leave it up to God by answering, "Sovereign Lord, you alone know" (verse 3). The command that God then gave must have taken Ezekiel by surprise: "Prophesy to these bones" (verse 4). The improbability of dead and scattered bones responding to a prophetic sermon only highlights the fact that this is a message with a promise from God, the Creator of all things.

But what possibly could be the meaning of this extraordinary message for the captives in Babylon and for us today? The promise in verse 5 is that God's breath will be placed in them and they will live. But how? Verse 6 provides the cryptic answer. God says, "I will attach tendons to you and make flesh come upon you and cover you with skin; I will put breath in you, and you will come to life."

Taking each of the elements of this promise as important to the understanding of the primary recipients of the prophecy, we now need to take each at face value. First of all, tendons are a type of connective tissue. Their role is to hold things together, namely bone to bone or bone to muscle. Could it be that the first step in God's formula for the revival of these scattered bones is couched here in a promise that He will draw them together?

The second element of this prophecy of revival is flesh. Flesh is most often associated with muscle. Bones that are strung together are useless without muscle fiber that provides viable opposing contractions and relaxations to produce movement and provide strength. For a powerless nation, convinced they have come to the end of their national identity, this promise of power provides hope that God has a purpose for them. Power and strength for the weak—what a gift!

The third element of this prophecy is skin. The skin is the largest organ of the body, with a total area of about twenty square feet. The skin protects us from microbes and other elements; it helps regulate body temperature and permits the sensations of touch, heat, and cold. This protective organ is wrapped around every part of the human body. It insulates the delicate muscle tissue that in turn protects the substantive organs of the body that, if left naked, would incur trauma, infection, and death.

After sin entered this world and infected human nature, God "made garments of skin for Adam and his wife and clothed them" (Genesis 3:21). Is it possible that the covering of skin that God offers to the captives in Babylon is similar to the garments of skin that He offered Adam and Eve? If so, could it be possible that God offers all humanity a covering of protective righteousness? And could this protective righteousness have something to do with the "white raiment" that Christ offers the church of Laodicea in the last days (Revelation 3:18, KJV)? Could it be?

The fourth element of this prophecy that offers hope to the scattered bones in this valley is the breath of God Himself—the infilling of the Spirit, the source of life itself. For these bones to become God's vast army, the Spirit must bring them to life. Just as Adam was formed from the dust of the ground and God breathed into him the breath of life and man became of living soul, or being (see Genesis 2:7), the Breath, or Spirit, is needed to fill each member of God's newly reconstituted army.

After this astounding experience, Ezekiel is reminded that it is not only God who knows if these bones will live. This experience now makes it common knowledge that God can revive that which is disconnected. God's people in captivity will live again and return to worship at His temple. The message of revival in Ezekiel 37 is God's conditional promise of resettling His revived people and reestablishing His temple (see verses 25–28).

Now that the captives in Babylon have the promise of their revival and restoration to their national identity as well as the reestablishment of God's temple, the question is, Revived for what? Revival is not enough! What is God's purpose in bringing them back to Jerusalem? How will God use a people whom He has reconstituted (Ezekiel 37) and to whom He has offered new hearts (Ezekiel 36:26)? Ezekiel 47 helps answer this question.

A river of life in a dead desert and sea

In Ezekiel 47, a new prophecy is given that looks ahead to an already reestablished temple in Jerusalem. In vision, Ezekiel saw God's temple in Jerusalem. God's presence had returned once again to His temple. But the temple appeared to have sprung a leak: "The man brought me back to the entrance to the temple, and I saw water coming out from under the threshold of the temple toward the east (for the temple faced east)" (Ezekiel 47:1).

If you look at a map of Ezekiel's part of the world, you will see that east of Jerusalem is the Salt Sea (also known as the Dead Sea because the high salt content prevents anything from living there), the lowest body of water on earth.

Between Jerusalem and the Dead Sea is approximately thirteen miles (twenty-two kilometers) of largely desert country. Ezekiel saw water flowing from under the threshold of the temple through the desert to the Dead Sea. In contrast to destructive rivers, we see that the river flowing from the temple is portrayed as the center and source of health and prosperity for the community.

However, for God's temple to be the source of health and prosperity for a community, the river that flows out has to come from a healthy, life-giving source within. Years after Ezekiel's prophecies, the prophet Zechariah declared that "a fountain will be opened to the house of David and the inhabitants of Jerusalem, to cleanse them from sin and impurity" (Zechariah 13:1).[1] Commenting on Zechariah 13:1, Ellen White says, "The waters of this fountain contain medicinal properties that will heal both physical and spiritual infirmities. From this fountain flows the mighty river seen in Ezekiel's vision [of Ezekiel 47]."[2]

One thousand cubits[3] from the temple, the water from the "leak" under the temple's threshold became "ankle-deep" (Ezekiel 47:3); and in subsequent similar measurements, the river from the temple was "knee-deep," waist deep (verse 4), and finally too deep to cross (verse 5).

Verses 6–9 contain a very exciting picture:

> He asked me, "Son of man, do you see this?"
>
> Then he led me back to the bank of the river. When I arrived there, I saw a great number of trees on each side of the river. He said to me, "This water flows toward the eastern region and goes down into the Arabah [a desert], where it enters the Dead Sea. When it empties into the sea, the salty water there becomes fresh. Swarms of living creatures will live wherever the river flows. There will be large numbers of fish, because this water flows there and makes the salt water fresh; so *where the river flows everything will live*" (emphasis added).

The river from the sanctuary flowed to the lowest spot on planet Earth, the Dead Sea. Do you sometimes feel like you live on the lowest spot on earth? Does sickness, financial struggle, divorce, or some other woe bring you or a loved one down low? The healing river goes there.

Wherever the river that flows from God's temple goes, there is life (verse 9)! What a testimony to the role of God's church! And, the river becomes deeper and wider until it enters the "Dead Sea."

But the "Dead Sea" is no longer dead. Verse 10 notes that there are fishermen along the shore of the formerly Dead Sea. The healing river creates an ideal environment for many fish. You say, "That's impossible! Nothing can live in the Dead Sea!" *But* nothing and no one are beyond the reach of God's grace.

Fishermen are part of this amazing story. We must be intentional about having effective fishermen in our church's ministry picture; otherwise, all we are doing is influencing the "fish." Because we are called to be "fishers of men" (Matthew 4:19, KJV), we must draw in these fish from the revitalized sea—inviting them to make a decision for Jesus—the Way, the Truth, and the Life (John 14:6).

The story continues in Ezekiel 47: "Fruit trees of all kinds will grow on both banks of the river. Their leaves will not wither, nor will their fruit fail. Every month they will bear fruit, because the water from the sanctuary flows to them. Their fruit will serve for food and their leaves for healing" (verse 12).

The trees that are sustained by the river will become nurturers and healers, too, bringing abundant life to those around them. The prophetic message also promises that someday God's people, whom He has healed and resurrected, will be transferred to the place where there is another river—the ultimate river flowing from the throne of God. There will be no deserts, no dryness, no death there. This is Eden restored, which also had a river of life in the beginning (Genesis 2:10).

For God's people in captivity, this was great news. Yet, we have the privilege of looking further into the future. In the apostle John's revelation of Jesus Christ, we read of the river of the water of life flowing from the throne of God (Revelation 22:1, 2).

The inhabitants of that fair land are described in Revelation 7:16, 17:

> " 'Never again will they hunger;
>   never again will they thirst.
> The sun will not beat down on them,'
>   nor any scorching heat.
> For the Lamb at the center of the throne
>   will be their shepherd;
> 'he will lead them to springs of living water.'
>   'And God will wipe away every tear from their eyes.' "

In the meantime, while we wait for that blessed reality, God wants our churches to be "river churches" from which flow healing and life to the community around us. He wants to work through us to revitalize and transform the deserts and Dead Seas in our territory. Jesus, through us, will come to the people around us and bring them abundant life

(John 10:10)—which is the wholistic Adventist message in a nutshell!

> Look at the past agendas and minutes of your church board. If they are primarily inwardly focused rather than "flowing outward" to bring wholistic healing to your neighborhood, it's time to change your way of thinking and your way of working!

---

1. Other Bible passages imply that when God's presence is in His people, they "will be . . . like a spring whose waters never fail" (Isaiah 58:11). Jesus calls the water He gives (through the church—His people) "living water" (John 4:10). "Whoever believes in me [Jesus], as Scripture has said, rivers of living water will flow from within them" (John 7:38).

2. Ellen G. White, *Testimonies for the Church* (Mountain View, CA: Pacific Press® Publishing Association, 1948), 6:227, 228.

3. A cubit is the first recorded unit of measurement and was used when people used their bodies as measuring devices. A cubit is generally the distance from the tips of one's fingers to the elbow—in other words, the forearm.

CHAPTER 5

Jesus on Community Outreach

Jesus of Nazareth had become so popular that the whole countryside was alerted to His ministry. As He went through Galilee, "in the power of the Spirit," He taught in synagogues, and "everyone praised him" (Luke 4:14, 15). He also healed every disease and sickness among the people. Large crowds from all over followed Him (Matthew 4:23–25).

The people of Nazareth could not ignore the fact that their hometown boy had become Somebody. So when Jesus came home and stopped in to worship at His home synagogue, the local leadership could not resist inviting Him to read the scriptures and comment on them. Curious about the rumors of Jesus' teaching, healing, and miraculous signs, the members of the congregation probably hoped that He would provide them with some evidence of His prowess.

With all eyes riveted on Him, Jesus accepts the scroll of the prophet Isaiah, finds chapter 61, and begins to read:

> The Spirit of the Sovereign LORD is on me,
>   because the LORD has anointed me
>   to proclaim good news to the poor.
> He has sent me to bind up the brokenhearted,
>   to proclaim freedom for the captives
>   and release from darkness for the prisoners,
> to proclaim the year of the LORD's favor (verses 1, 2).

Jesus then stops abruptly in midsentence, leaving out the phrase "and the day of vengeance of our God" (verse 2).[1] Contrary to the common teaching about the role of the Messiah, Jesus had come to earth at His first advent as a Savior, Healer, and Restorer, not to be at the head of an army that would conquer and bring vengeance upon the oppressive Romans.[2] At His second advent, He will come as a Judge (2 Thessalonians 1:5–11) and thus fulfill the rest of Isaiah 61:2.

Proclaiming the "year of the LORD's favor" was significant to the people of Jesus' time. Also known as "a jubilee" (Leviticus 25:10), this fiftieth year was sacred. Jubilee was a time of freedom and of celebration, when everyone would receive back their original property; debts were forgiven; slaves could return home to their families; and prisoners would be released. However, "there is no record in the Bible, or outside it, of an actual observance of the jubilee."[3] The reading of Isaiah 61 was, to those in the synagogue that Sabbath, known as a Messianic passage because it was believed that the Messiah would usher in the jubilee.

After Jesus read from Isaiah, with all eyes on Him, Jesus sat down to preach and assured them, "Today this scripture is fulfilled in your hearing" (Luke 4:21).[4] Strangely, the revelation that Jesus was the fulfillment of the jubilee did not appear to bother the attendees at the synagogue at first. Luke 4:22 says, "All spoke well of him and were amazed at the gracious words that came from his lips." But how could this be? Who was this Man whom they thought they knew from long ago? The minds of those who were listening in the synagogue that day struggled to reconcile the rumors surrounding Jesus' birth with this revelation of Jesus' Messianic role in restoring the jubilee.

Their doubts turned to violent anger against Jesus when He pointed out the fact that, in the past, God's blessings and healing were sometimes withheld from His people and were shared with the heathen and the Gentiles—the Sidonian widow of Zarephath and Naaman, the Syrian general (verses 25–28). The Jews reacted ferociously when Jesus highlighted catering to people who were "outsiders." Selfishness had prevented them from experiencing the jubilee and also had prevented them from reaching out to outsiders.

Jesus' teachings and ministry methods were radical and departed from the status quo, especially when it came to relating to outsiders. What is your attitude about connecting with outsiders? Are there any prejudices that keep you from doing so? The following is what one church decided to do.

Brazilian Seventh-day Adventist Central Church reaches out to visiting youth

In August 2013, Seventh-day Adventist Church members in Rio de Janeiro "demonstrated Christian hospitality" after discovering that 170 Catholic youth from Italy would be in their city for World Youth Day.

> The Italian Catholics were part of the World Youth Day Pilgrimage, which saw thousands of young Catholics worldwide travel to Rio de Janeiro for a week to celebrate the diversity of the Catholic Church and deepen their personal spirituality.
>
> Members of the Adventist Central Church in Rio de Janeiro welcomed the group at the airport and provided transportation and accommodation at the church during their week oft pilgrimage.
>
> "We have our doctrinal differences, but we serve a God who gave us an example of loving our neighbors. We are helping these young people not because of their faith, but because they are in need and we would assist members of any denomination," said Romulo Silva, a local church leader.
>
> During the week . . . , local Adventist churches also took the opportunity to pray for the young Catholics and invite them to local church functions.
>
> "Several of the [young people] wanted to join in our worship every night and said they liked what they heard," Silva said, adding that he believes kindness and generosity can send a stronger message than preaching.[5]

These church members understood that their neighbor is *anyone* who needs help. This was a major teaching of Jesus.

Two men, one question

At two different times during Jesus' ministry, two men approached Him with the same question. In Luke 10:25, we meet an "expert in the law": " 'Teacher,' he asked, 'what must I do to inherit eternal life?' "

Jesus responds by asking the man what the law says, and the man correctly says to love God with all our heart, soul, and strength, and our neighbor as ourselves. A question then arises: "And who is my neighbor?" (verse 29). In response, Jesus shares the story of a Samaritan who chooses to meet the needs of a wounded Jew on the road to Jericho. This ignorant Samaritan was closer to the kingdom of God than the religious priest and the Levite who both passed by the wounded man, choosing not to defile themselves because of the godly work they were called to do. They likely asked themselves, "What will happen to me if I help?" A better question would have been, "What will happen to him (the needy one) if I don't help?" The issue is not who my neighbor is. Rather, it is, Am I a neighbor to those in need? God prefers our compassion over our religious zeal (Proverbs 21:3).

In Luke 18:18–30, Jesus meets a rich ruler who asks, "Good teacher, what must I do to inherit eternal life?" (verse 18). Jesus answers, "You know the commandments: 'You shall not commit adultery, you shall not murder, you shall not steal, you shall not give false testimony, honor your father and mother' " (verse 20). The rich ruler rejoices in being able to claim that he has done these things. Wholehearted, unselfish caring for the needs of the less fortunate is a crucial part of following Jesus; and the ruler is certain that he has kept this part of the law. However, Jesus informs this young ruler that he still lacks one thing (verse 22). The young man is now confronted with the first part of the law—loving the Lord with all his heart and having no other gods to hinder the relationship. To this young ruler, going through the motions of loving his neighbor is easier than actually loving God above all else—including his wealth.

Both the expert in the law and the rich young ruler asked the same question. The expert in the law had trouble understanding the concept of his neighbor being anyone who needs a neighbor, including strangers and outsiders. He thus disqualified himself from following Jesus in ministry beyond Judaism. The rich young ruler, on the other hand, had trouble with his total commitment to Jesus. To reach a full understanding on how to love God wholeheartedly, total surrender required that he sell everything.

In Matthew's account of the story, Jesus reminds the rich young ruler, "If you want to be perfect, go, sell your possessions and give to the poor, and you will have treasure in heaven. Then come, follow me" (Matthew 19:21). In the Sermon on the Mount, in the context of showing love for anyone—even outsiders and enemies—Jesus told His audience to "be perfect, therefore, as your heavenly Father is perfect" (Matthew 5:48). A parallel passage in Luke 6:36 says, "Be merciful, just as your Father is merciful." Therefore, perfection and mercy are related.

Good neighbors in Washington, DC: Fourth Street Friendship Seventh-day Adventist Church demonstrates perfect and merciful love

Every Sunday, before the sun rises, volunteers are at the pancake house at Fourth Street Friendship Seventh-day Adventist Church in Washington, DC—seven blocks from the United States Capitol. The volunteers have come to prepare a delicious breakfast for the neighbors of the church who are homeless and hungry.

Jesse Reaves and his wife, Mary, established a soup kitchen at Fourth Street Friendship in 1973 to create a church that would be an accessible and welcoming place in their community. They served meals on Sunday when most other soup kitchens were closed.

Later on, Louis Williams was impressed to organize the Bread of Life Ministry—a church service—for those who came to their soup kitchen/pancake house for breakfast. Guests have two food options: physical food as well as spiritual food from the Word of God. This Adventist Community Services outreach at Fourth Street Friendship is now a multichurch, multidenominational ministry, which volunteers have been coming to for decades.

Fourth Street Friendship endeavors to help the whole person—physically, mentally, socially, and spiritually. There is a medical ministry with health education seminars conducted by physical and mental health professionals. There are also ongoing substance abuse support groups.

Through a grant from the North American Division Adventist Community Services, the church started a computer skills class to provide foundational training for those interested in a computer career. The class also provides access to the Web, allowing clients to search for jobs; build an online presence with e-mail, résumés, and profiles in order to find work; and secure housing to become self-sufficient again.

The church has touched hundreds of thousands of lives since it began its service in the community more than forty years ago. This is epitomized in the story of Larry Bryant, a drug addict living in a homeless shelter. Twenty years ago his bunkmate at a homeless shelter invited him to come to Fourth Street Friendship for breakfast. Larry met Jesus there; and now he is employed, married, and living in a home in suburban Maryland. He has been drug-free for more than fifteen years, and he is the head deacon at the Fourth Street Friendship church. Once a month he preaches at the Bread of Life Ministry.

The community around Fourth Street Friendship is gentrifying currently, so the church is adapting its ministry to meet the latest needs. Therefore, Fourth Street Friendship is focusing more on technology instead of food (although they continue to provide Sunday-morning breakfasts). They installed a tower that gives their community free Wi-Fi in exchange for viewing messages about events at the church. At the time of this writing, at least "1,500 neighbors have logged on and become aware of the church, causing Andrew Harwood, former senior pastor, to conclude, 'We have to think in terms of unique relevance. It used to be about soup and sandwiches; now it's about technology.' "

With a church located every three or four blocks in their community, the members of Fourth Street Friendship were motivated to "offer something that the other churches were not offering." Pastor Harwood said, "Now we can go into their homes," adding that he has several followers on his personal Twitter account because of the Internet service.[6]

Samples of other teachings that Jesus preached and practiced

The Fourth Street Friendship church reflects Jesus, who practiced His own teachings with His own methods of doing ministry (Matthew 9:35–38). For example, as Jesus mingled with the people, showed sympathy, and ministered to their needs, He demonstrated the meaning of His teachings about the salt of the earth (Matthew 5:13), the light of the world (verse 14), the golden rule (Matthew 7:12), the farmer who planted seeds on different soils (Matthew 13), and much more.[7]

Salt of the earth. In this passage, Jesus is calling His followers to be "salt," which is a transforming agent. Salt makes food taste better, melts ice, preserves (saves), creates thirst, heals—the list goes on. The church is a "saltshaker" that contains the "salt of the earth" (Matthew 5:13). Jesus modeled this idea as He spent time outside the comfort zone of His Jewish heritage—with sinners and foreigners of various kinds. He improved their quality of lives (John 10:10); "melted ice" between Himself and supposed enemies; created a thirst for something better (such as with the Samaritan woman in John 4); and healed and saved people wholistically, such as the paralytic (Mark 2:1–12). "For the Son of Man came to seek and to save the lost" (Luke 19:10).

Jesus doesn't call us to be only salt but savory salt—that has not lost its savor (Matthew 5:13). On the surface, the two look the same. Those who have lost their *savor,* however, have lost connection with their *Savior,* and are like the world, as implied in Psalm 106:35, 36. God's people, Israel,

> mingled with the nations
> and adopted their customs.
> They worshiped their idols,
> which became a snare to them.

To make a difference in this world, we must be different in a positive, balanced, Christlike way, as we mingle with those different from ourselves.

Light of the world and golden rule. Jesus showed the meaning of His teaching about being the light of the world when He pierced through the darkness of people's lives, sometimes literally by healing the blind. He also opened the eyes of the spiritually blind to see the light by reminding them of their very surroundings—the obvious around them that they did not seem to see. He said, "The poor you will always have with you" (Mark 14:7). In other words, do not miss this obvious reality. It is all around you, and you are missing it. You will always be among the poor and can always help them.[8]

Dwight Nelson, referring to Jesus' golden rule in Matthew 7:12, asks, "Could it be that *the poor are our golden opportunity to exercise the golden rule?*"[9] This golden echo from Christ's sermon on the mount has powerful implications for His church today: "When those who profess the name of Christ shall practice the principles of the golden rule, the same power will attend the gospel as in apostolic times."[10]

Church planting and the parable of the farmer planting seeds. The story in Matthew 13 of the farmer planting seeds on all kinds of soils illustrates the role of Christ's church. Yes, we must share the seed ("the message about the kingdom" [verse 19]) with all types of soil (people). However, gospel farmers may be tempted to complain that their neighborhood field does not have adequate good ground, and there is too much hard, rocky, thorny ground. But this undesirable soil is a calling for the church to proactively change the quality of the soil in its community! Community services can prepare more good soil by softening the hard ground and removing the rocks (removing barriers, softening hard hearts, and so on through trusting relationships formed in the community) and the thorns (removing people's worries, cares, and distractions [verse 22] by helping them with these problems and pointing them to better heavenly treasures). Then there will be more good ground for "the message about the kingdom."

We often hear about church planting. Instead of focusing on merely planting churches on good ground, it is better to plant a ministry and grow a church out of a ministry. A ministry should be dedicated to preparing good ground from ground that has hardness, rocks, and thorns. When you only focus on planting a church, often the emphasis is on the church itself. When you plant a serving-the-community ministry first, the resulting church will likely be focused on ministry.

Southern Asia-Pacific Division's administrative office's Adventist Community Services

The culture of local community ministry can show itself not only in a local church, but in other interesting places. For example, the administrative office of the vast Southern Asia-Pacific Division (SSD) of the Seventh-day Adventist Church in Silang, Cavite, Philippines, hired Luz Villanueva as a full-time Adventist Community Services director to lead the office staff in serving the needy community around the SSD office. Activities so far include a day care; a feeding program; marriage counseling in Silang's municipal office; a jail ministry; a senior citizen ministry, providing wheelchairs; and much more. Whenever Luz visits the mayor's office, the mayor says, "I like it when you come to my office, because you bring service, not problems."

May God help all Seventh-day Adventist institutions and churches to have such reputations in their surrounding communities! This will happen if you and I do community outreach as Jesus did—"everyone praised him" (Luke 4:15).

> Think of someone outside your comfort zone. Endeavor to connect with him or her as Jesus might have done if He met that person.

1. See and compare Luke 4:17–20.

2. See Ellen G. White, *The Desire of Ages* (Mountain View, CA: Pacific Press® Publishing Association, 1940), 236.

3. Siegfried H. Horn, *Seventh-day Adventist Bible Dictionary* (Hagerstown, MD: Review and Herald® Publishing Association, 1979), 625.

4. Preachers preached sitting down back then.

5. Adventist News Network, "In Brazil, Adventists Demonstrate Christian Hospitality," Adventist New Network bulletin, August 1, 2013, http://news.adventist.org/all-news/news /go/2013-08-01/in-brazil-adventists-demonstrate-christian-hospitality/.

6. Adapted from "Washington, D.C., Church Provides Wi-Fi to Neighborhood," Columbia Union *Visitor,* March 26, 2014, accessed September 29, 2015, http://www .columbiaunionvisitor.com/washington-d-c-church-provides-wi-fi-to-neighborhood/ and Adventist Community Services, "To Touch a Life," online video, 6:06, accessed September 29, 2015, featuring Fourth Street Friendship, produced by the North American Division Adventist Community Services, http://www.communityservices.org/featured-videos/.

7. See White, *The Ministry of Healing,* 143.

8. See Mark R. Gornik, *To Live in Peace: Biblical Faith and the Changing Inner City* (Grand Rapids, MI: Eerdmans, 2002), 6.

9. Dwight Nelson, *Pursuing the Passion of Jesus* (Nampa, ID: Pacific Press® Publishing Association, 2005), 56; emphasis in original.

10. Ellen G. White, *Thoughts From the Mount of Blessing* (Mountain View, CA: Pacific Press® Publishing Association, 1956), 137.

CHAPTER 6

Jesus Mingled With People

Creative mingling—Brazilian surf and skateboard community

Pastor Vinicius Metzker loves to surf offshore in the state of São Paulo, Brazil. He mingles and makes friends with many surfers who share his passion for surfing. But he doesn't just catch waves; from time to time, he catches his surfer friends' attention while he sits atop his surfboard and reads to them choice verses from his special waterproof Bible. This surfboard "congregation" gathers around Pastor Vinicius as he leads them in a Bible study, passing his waterproof Bible around from surfboard to surfboard in the deep water. He then invites his wet friends to his church.

On other days, Pastor Vinicius can be seen skateboarding with young people in his community—surfing on dry ground. He also started a motorcycle club. Between his surfing, skateboarding, and motorcycling, Pastor Vinicius has taken mingling to a new and creative level, making several friends from his "missionary playtime."

Pastor Vinicius also pastors a church close to the shore, with more than two hundred attendees—a faith community of mostly surfers and skateboarders. About ten of the surfers are baptized. Like Jesus, Pastor Vinicius does whatever it takes to connect with the people where they are, so that he can befriend and save them.

Jesus, the Master Mingler

What might it have been like to sit near the marketplace close to the center of town and hear the commotion of the townspeople as they pressed around Jesus? Mothers scurrying along with a baby or two, eager to have Jesus bless their offspring; beloved friends aiding a sick neighbor to the feet of Jesus; rabbis testing out their latest schemes to entrap Jesus on some point of doctrine, oral law, or custom; outcasts eager to verify rumors that this man welcomes those who are marginalized in society. How would it be to get caught up in the excitement of meeting a Person who is more eager to care than to judge? What would it take to find Someone who is willing to spend special time with you even when there are those around warning Him not to defile Himself with you? This is the Jesus we meet in Luke 15:1, 2—a Man who surrounds Himself with tax collectors and sinners and gets accused of welcoming sinners and eating with them.

In Matthew 9:35–38, we read about Jesus' ministry in "all the towns and villages" as He compassionately mingled, preached, and healed. After advising the disciples to pray that more workers[1] be sent to His harvest field, we see how Jesus actually sent out workers. In Matthew 10:5–10, Jesus counsels His disciples to (1) start where you are currently located (don't go to the Gentiles or Samaritans until you have ministered to those closest to you);[2] (2) preach that the blessings of the kingdom of heaven start here and now; (3) heal people and cast out demons; and (4) do not take anything with you that would guarantee your self-sufficiency, because if you do not bring supplies you must create relationships in the neighborhood to meet your organization's needs as you serve the community. The ministry of Jesus and His disciples began by mingling with people at every opportunity and circumstance.

The scribes and Pharisees thought it strange that Jesus, a Man who claimed such spiritual authority, would stoop so low as to mingle and identify so closely with the common riffraff of society. Most authority figures stand apart from the crowd; Roman and Greek conquerors drew personal attention and insisted on creating a barrier of respect and aloofness. Instead, Jesus commanded respect as He stood shoulder to shoulder with common people.

Should it have surprised them so much that He who claimed to be the One sent from God would behave that way? God has always sought to be in the midst of His people. He fellowshiped and walked with Adam and Eve in the Garden of Eden. When Adam and Eve sinned, He sought to go where they were, even though they were hiding from Him. Generation after generation of God's faithful were praised for their walk with God (as in the case of Enoch; Genesis 5:24). When guiding His people to the Promised Land, God made His presence felt in the pillar of cloud by day, which turned into a pillar of fire by night. In the midst of the journey, God commanded that the Israelites build a sanctuary for Him so He could dwell among them (Exodus 25:8). The plan of salvation revealed in the sanctuary services reminded God's people of His plan to separate them from sin through confession of sin and a substitutionary sacrifice that would eliminate the sin barrier that separated the people from Him. God's plan was to provide atonement through the substitutionary death of an innocent lamb. Later, during the Babylonian captivity, God impressed His people with the promise that "you will be my people, and I will be your God" (Ezekiel 36:28). God's promises and miraculous leadings in the rebuilding of the temple in Jerusalem reflected His persistent desire to dwell with His people.

Four centuries later, "when the fulness of the time was come," an angel announced to Joseph that Mary would bear a son (Galatians 4:4, KJV). This Jesus would come in fulfillment of the prophecy in Isaiah 7:14: "The virgin will conceive and give birth to a son, and will call him Immanuel [which means God with us]." Throughout the gospel story, the life and ministry of Jesus continued to reflect God's passion for mingling with people and giving them access to grace and forgiveness of sin. Jesus made Himself available to sinners with an open invitation to all who labor and are heavy laden to come to Him and find rest (see Matthew 11:28). "God sent His Son into the world that He might learn by actual experience the needs of humanity."[3]

When accused by onlookers of welcoming sinners and eating with them (Luke 15:1, 2), Jesus told three parables to help the self-centered critics understand His motives. A shepherd lovingly seeks the one sheep that was lost because "there will be more rejoicing in heaven over one sinner who repents than over ninety-nine righteous persons who do not need to repent" (verse 7). A woman searches carefully throughout her house to find a lost coin because "there is rejoicing in the presence of the angels of God over one sinner who repents" (verse 10). A father waits eagerly for his lost son and celebrates his arrival because "this [son] . . . was dead and is alive again; he was lost and is found" (verse 32). God does whatever it takes to find the lost ones who are separated from Him. It matters not where the lost are located. They could have wandered out of the church (the parable of the lost sheep); they could be in the house—in the church (the parable of the lost coin); or they could have rebelliously left the church and gone into the world (the parable of the lost son).

In John 17, we read that Jesus prayed for His disciples: "My prayer is not that you take them out of the world but that you protect them from the evil one. . . . As you sent me into the world, I have sent them into the world" (verses 15, 18). One theologian, in commenting on this passage, concluded that every disciple of Christ needs two conversions: (1) from the world to Christ, and (2) back into the world with Christ.[4]

God has called His church to reflect the mission that He was sent into the world to accomplish—to mingle with people in ways that demonstrate the love of God, which sent Jesus into the world (John 3:16). We need His attitude of reaching out in order to draw near to the people in our neighborhoods, opening the way for God's grace to enter into the immediate context of society. We need to go beyond praying from a distance:

> He who does nothing but pray will soon cease to pray, or his prayers will become a formal routine. When men take themselves out of social life, away from the sphere of Christian duty and cross bearing; when they cease to work earnestly for the Master, who worked earnestly for them, they lose the subject matter of prayer and have no incentive to devotion. Their prayers become personal and selfish. They cannot pray in regard to the wants of humanity or the upbuilding of Christ's kingdom, pleading for strength wherewith to work.[5]

In the midst of mingling with those who have yet to know Christ, each of us must remember who and whose we are. We are the salt that must not lose its distinctive flavor (Matthew 5:13). We are the light that shines best when in the darkness (verse 14). "Do everything without grumbling or arguing, so that you may become blameless and pure, 'children of God without fault in a warped and crooked generation.' Then you will shine among them like stars in the sky" (Philippians 2:14, 15).

Jesus mingled with a purpose. He does not intend for His mingling followers to fit into the mold of the world.[6] Rather, He calls each of us to be intentional in our connection with Him, so that the light and atmosphere of heaven can shine through us in a world of darkness.

Central Coast Community Church—an incarnational church

The Central Coast Community Church (CCCC) in Wyong, New South Wales, Australia, is committed to incarnational ministry, by being a bright light in a dark neighborhood, through unreservedly connecting with its unchurched community for Christ. This Adventist congregation worships on Sabbath in a community center with a skateboard park. The center was built by the local government to help curb the high suicide rate and unemployment in the neighborhood by giving troubled and troublesome youth a place to hang out. Several denominations were offered the use of the center to foster a moral influence there. The only church group that said Yes was CCCC. This was the exact group CCCC wanted to reach, so the church happily moved into the community center. The members sincerely believed that "it is through the social relations that Christianity comes in contact with the world."[7]

The members and Pastor Wayne Krause believe that working in and working with the neighborhood are just as important as working in their local church. Pastor Krause says, "My church is a place for those who are not here yet." When people from the community do attend their church, they make it a place where all are made welcome and shown love and forgiveness—yes—even "sinners."

CCCC has three members who were involved in witchcraft, one former satanic priestess, and at least one ex-prostitute. There is a Sabbath School class that is a smoking class. It started by accident with people who felt accepted at their church even though they smoked. Because the community youth center where the church meets is a public area (where smoking is not allowed), the smokers would gather in an outside gazebo to smoke. Someone noticed this and started a Sabbath School class there. Many former members of the smokers class no longer smoke and are now church members.

Nathan, a heroin addict, approached two women who belonged to

CCCC and asked them to take him to the methadone clinic. After taking him to the clinic, one of the women took him home and fed him. The CCCC got him an apartment, and members were a support to him. Later Nathan was arrested. In court, Nathan's mother met three men from CCCC who had been a support to him. She thanked them for all they and CCCC had done for her son.

Nathan's family wanted to meet the pastor of CCCC. Six family members who were part of a heavy metal group drove three hours and walked into CCCC one Sabbath morning. They were a rough-looking bunch—with tattoos, all kinds of piercings, and leather jackets. They wanted to see what kind of church would help their brother. They paraded down the aisle to the front after the worship service had started; no one in the congregation flinched. Pastor Wayne changed his sermon on the spot to the great controversy theme. After the sermon, Nathan's family members talked to Pastor Wayne. They said, "We've never been in a church." Wayne's great controversy sermon had really touched them, and they realized they are in the middle of a war in which they are the prizes. Wayne gave each of them a Bible. One of them, the lead singer in the heavy metal band, clasped the Bible, holding it carefully; this was his first Bible. These six asked, "How can we learn more about this?" Wayne said, "Come back next week." And they kept coming. Now they are taking Bible studies and are preparing to be baptized.

Starting with three individuals, this church grew to three hundred in five years; around 20 percent of the people on any given Sabbath will be unchurched. In addition, six churches have been planted by people from CCCC. All CCCC members, both those who transfer in from other Adventist churches and newly baptized members, sign a covenant of commitment to their church after attending a membership class. Part of that covenant is that they will be part of a small group, be nonjudgmental to everyone they meet in their community and who comes through the door of their church, and be involved in a ministry in the community. The church leadership encourages members to join existing organizations in the community, providing another opportunity for mingling.

The church itself has initiated various services for their community. For example, after assessing their community, they discovered that a school nearby has many at-risk students who come to school without breakfast. Therefore, for several years, CCCC has provided breakfasts at this public school, in partnership with Sanitarium Foods and the Red Cross. Later, after the Australian government made provision for public schools to have chaplains, this school asked CCCC to provide a chaplain from their membership, and CCCC did so. Ministries to the community continue to be added, such as Relationship Plus, a support group that helps individuals and couples work through addictions and relationship problems. A strong men's group, called Valiant Man, helps men in areas of sexuality and provides male role models.

Pastor Krause has what he calls his office at a coffee shop in the local shopping mall in town. He spends quite a bit of time there counseling, giving Bible studies, and running a small group. The people who run the coffee shop take appointments for him, and he has been asked to do some weddings for the staff. One employee has attended CCCC, and the owner of the coffee shop has jokingly said he will put a cross on one of the tables so people will know Pastor Wayne is there.

CCCC has been mingling with the marginalized and the undesirable, just like Jesus did.

> Though He was a Jew, Christ mingled with the Samaritans, setting at naught the Pharisaic customs of His nation. In face of their prejudices, He accepted the hospitality of this despised people. He slept under their roofs, ate with them at their tables, partaking of the food prepared and served by their hands—and taught in their streets, and treated them with the utmost kindness and courtesy.[8]

Are there any "Samaritans" in your neighborhood who need to meet you? Can they, as did the apostle John, say the following about the Jesus they see in you—because you are close enough for them to notice?

> The Word became flesh and blood,
>> and moved into the neighborhood.
> We saw the glory with our own eyes,
>> the one-of-a-kind glory,
>> like Father, like Son, [like Son, like you?]
> Generous inside and out,
>> true from start to finish (John 1:14, *The Message*).

Make an intentional plan to mingle with a mission with a person or a group in your community you haven't related to before. Then do it!

1. Not only reapers, by the way.

2. Another reason Jesus instructed His disciples not to go to the Gentiles and Samaritans was to avoid unnecessary prejudice from the Jews at this point in His ministry. Also, the disciples were unprepared to work with Gentiles. A year later, when the Seventy were sent out, they began their labor among the Samaritans. See Ellen G. White, *The Desire of Ages,* 488. Also see *The Seventh-day Adventist Bible Commentary,* ed. F. D. Nichol (Hagerstown, MD: Review and Herald® Publishing Association, 1980), 5:375.

3. Ellen G. White, *Ministry to the Cities* (Hagerstown, MD: Review and Herald® Publishing Association, 2012), 59.

4. Sometimes credited to John Stott.

5. Ellen G. White, *Steps to Christ* (Washington, DC: Review and Herald® Publishing Association, 1956), 101.

6. Psalm 106:35–39 shows examples of how *not* to mingle.

7. White, *The Ministry of Healing,* 496.

8. Ellen G. White, *Selected Messages* (Hagerstown, MD: Review and Herald® Publishing Association, 1980), bk. 3, 238.

CHAPTER

Jesus Desired Their Good

Rebellion, celebration, and rebellion against celebration

Eli steps to the edge of the plowed field, brooding over all the time that he has to spend helping maintain his father's farm estate and all the logistics associated with it. His younger brother, Jake, forced the distribution of his father's inheritance to both sons (Luke 15:12), absconded with Jake's own portion of the proceeds, and went to the Gentiles. Eli feels a degree of rueful satisfaction that the community at large has relegated Jake to censure and banishment through the tradition of the *cherem,* which renders Jake as a nonperson and dead to the fellowship of the faithful.

Now his father wastes time standing on the veranda of the house each day, scanning the horizon looking for signs of Jake's return. *Doesn't Dad realize he must put Jake's memory behind him and come to grips with the reality that Jake can never come back as his son? Can't he simply rest in the assurance that Jake will never again disgrace the sanctity of the family name?* Eli rolls his eyes at the fact that he himself is still giving thought to this. After all, Jake is dead.

As the sun sets, Eli tiredly lumbers off toward the family compound and hears music and merriment coming from the main house. Surprised that a party would be taking place on a weekday and noting that he has not been notified of this event, Eli summons a servant and asks what is happening. The reply shakes Eli to the core: " 'Your brother has come,' [the servant] replied, 'and your father has killed the fattened calf because he has him back safe and sound' " (verse 27). Angered and disgusted by this travesty of justice—this total disregard of *cherem* that will now call into question the integrity of the family—this public display of weakness and compromise, Eli refuses to enter the celebration.

Eli walks toward his living quarters, dusk casting long shadows in his path. His father, having heard of Eli's anger, hurriedly approaches with a pleading look on his face. Raising his hand to stop his father's plea, Eli blurts out his pent-up frustrations. "All these years I have stayed by you! I've been obedient! You have not called for a celebration for me! Now this son of yours shows up and you make a fuss? He doesn't count! Have you lost your mind? Send him to the slave quarters if you must, but Jake is not my brother!"

The father, wounded to the core, seeks to reason with Eli: " 'My son,' . . . 'you are always with me, and everything I have is yours. But we had to celebrate and be glad, because this brother of *yours* was dead and is alive again; he was lost and is found' " (verses 31, 32; emphasis added).

In more modern times, Gaspar and some of his Jewish friends were visiting a synagogue in his neighborhood. In one of the meeting rooms, they noticed a group of people gathered for what appeared to be a funeral. Gaspar asked one of his friends, "Who died?" His friend explained they were holding a *cherem* ceremony (similar to a funeral) for a Jewish girl who was physically alive but was dead as far as the family was concerned. Why? She had married a Gentile.

Do we have the attitude of wishing the sinners around us were dead? Or would we rather wish them well and introduce them to Jesus, the One who longs to make them alive (Ephesians 2:5) and give them an abundant life (John 10:10)?

The worth of a soul

God unconditionally loves and values people—the faithful and the rebellious. Instead of imposing *cherem* when we rebel, He celebrates when we return to Him (Luke 15:7).

Every person is valuable to God for at least two reasons: First, God created humankind (and He does not make junk); after all, He created us in His image (Genesis 1:26, 27; 2:7). The second reason is that He paid a high price to redeem us (John 3:16). Because He loves us, "God

. . . made us alive with Christ even when we were dead in transgressions—it is by grace you have been saved" (Ephesians 2:4, 5). What a contrast—"made us alive" instead of making us dead, as in *cherem*!

The elder brother did not desire the good of his wayward brother, who was worthless and worse than dead to him. This supposedly "unrebellious" brother was still in good standing in the family, and he could not care less about what happened to his rebellious brother who was made dead. However, when his repentant brother returned, the older brother also became rebellious because of the joyful celebration for the return of his brother, who had experienced *cherem.*

How about modern-day church members who have stayed in the family of God? It is a sobering reality that "many who profess His name have lost sight of the fact that Christians are to represent Christ. Unless there is practical self-sacrifice for the good of others, in the family circle, in the neighborhood, in the church, and wherever we may be, then whatever our profession, we are not Christians."[1]

Desiring the good of those inside the church

Do we place a high worth on people—others and ourselves? Do we unselfishly desire the good of those in our church family, even if they stray sometime? "As Christ had loved them, the disciples were to love one another. They were to show forth the love abiding in their hearts for men, women, and children, by doing all in their power for their salvation. *But they were to reveal a specially tender love for all of the same faith.*"[2]

Dwight Nelson points out that this was the secret of the explosive growth of the early Christian church. Their unselfish love and care for each other became "their most potent evangelistic strategy."[3] The inner Christian community was living proof of the impact of God's grace, and it attracted those in the community outside the church to be part of it. "See how these Adventist Christians love and care for one another." "A specially tender love for all of the same faith."[4] After all, who would not want to join a church that is like that?[5]

The Triadelphia Seventh-day Adventist Church in Clarksville, Maryland, U.S.A., shows unselfish care for their young people by mailing care packages at the beginning of each school year to all the students who are attending school away from home. Church members donate the contents of these care packages, which contain school supplies, some home-baked goodies, and other expressions of love and caring. The away-from-home students receive them with joy. Often their friends wish they belonged to a church like that. This church also has a Prayers and Squares quilting group that makes quilts to show care and love to the ill and discouraged inside and outside their church. As church members tie each knot on the quilt, they say a prayer for the person receiving the quilt. Those people delivering the quilts tell the recipients that each knot on the quilt represents a prayer for them.

Desiring the good of those outside the church

The people of Sodom and Gomorrah were definitely outsiders. One could not be more outside of God's people than being from Sodom and Gomorrah. The extreme wickedness of these "cities of the plain" (Genesis 19:29) and Abraham's intercession on behalf of these wicked outsiders are portrayed in Genesis 18:16–33 and chapter 19. Abraham's nephew, Lot, lived there with his wife and children. But Abraham desired the good of not only his relatives. At first, he pled with God to save the city if there were fifty righteous people (Genesis 18:23, 24). God also desired the good of the people in the wicked city of Sodom and wanted to find a way to save them. "The LORD said, 'If I find fifty righteous people in the city of Sodom, I will spare the whole place for their sake' " (verse 26). To give Sodom a better chance of not being destroyed, Abraham negotiated down to saving the city if only ten people were righteous (verse 32).

"Love for perishing souls inspired Abraham's prayer. While he loathed the sins of that corrupt city, he desired that the sinners might be saved. His deep interest for Sodom shows the anxiety that we should feel for the impenitent. We should cherish hatred of sin, but pity and love for the sinner."[6]

God showed His concern for the good of other heathen peoples mentioned in Scripture, such as the city of Nineveh (Jonah 4:11) and Babylon, when He asked His people who were exiled in Babylon to "seek the peace and prosperity [Hebrew *Shalom*] of the city to which I have carried you into exile. Pray to the LORD for it" (Jeremiah 29:7). *Shalom* means complete peace, wholeness in every way—physically, mentally, socially, and spiritually.

What needs to happen in your heart and in your church to truly desire the good of the village, the town, the city, and the people therein around you, even though they may be considered wicked, involved in crime, and so forth? The lyrics of a gospel song are "I'm so glad Jesus lifted me!" Do we focus only on *me* in that song, or do we desire that Jesus would lift up others too? Below are three examples of Adventist groups who unselfishly care for the good of others.

The unselfish caring of the Stillwater Seventh-day Adventist Church

The Far Hills Seventh-day Adventist Church, founded in the late 1800s, was the first and mother church of all the congregations in the Dayton, Ohio, U.S.A., area. By 1980, the church was declining. The remnant of this Adventist congregation moved into a new neighborhood in the northern suburbs of Dayton to minister to families in response to a demographic study done by Monte Sahlin. They took the name *Stillwater Seventh-day Adventist Church.* The church members unselfishly turned their eyes outward to their church's neighborhood. They didn't have a sanctuary in which to worship at first, so they rented two facilities until their current building was built. The good of the community was their priority, so they first built the fellowship and community section of the facility.

They opened a community day-care center to help provide child care for their busy working neighbors. The center opened with half a dozen children, and today there are more than one hundred children enrolled—95 percent of them are community kids.

The Stillwater church continued to grow and, in 2005, completed phase two of the construction of the twenty-four-thousand-square-foot facility, which included a new sanctuary, classrooms, and a community room. The church originally moved north with sixty-five individuals; as of 2014, there are 155 members.

Community engagement is a priority at Stillwater, which is demonstrated in its partnerships with a number of local ministries and its participation in numerous community activities. These projects include the Oasis House ministry, which ministers to women working in strip clubs in Dayton; the city of Vandalia, which does rehabs on homes that have been cited for zoning violations; the Artemis Center for battered women; visiting the Dayton Children's Hospital emergency rooms with goodies for parents and children; participating in national rebuilding projects in the city of Dayton; participating in community picnics;

sponsoring annual health fairs; conducting community health classes on diabetes and stress management; and serving as a Red Cross disaster center in the event of a community emergency. In addition, Stillwater partners with the Good Neighbor House, a Seventh-day Adventist Community Services center in downtown Dayton, by providing volunteers, financial support, and leadership on the board.

Beth-el Seventh-day Adventist Church

Another example of unselfish caring for the good of others is Beth-el Seventh-day Adventist Church, a church plant in Jersey City, New Jersey, U.S.A. The culture of ministry was strong in the members from the outset. However, they had a challenge to surmount: they needed a church home. The congregation decided not to buy a church building for themselves; instead, they bought a storefront situated near the locale in which 95 percent of them lived so they could better minister to their neighborhood.

The church is part of the community, and the community is part of the church. They desired to be open seven days a week, not just on Sabbath. For them, church is not just coming once per week to worship. They do not want to be merely religious practitioners. Instead, they aspire to impact their neighborhood all week. For them, "church" is a community of believers who do not exist for themselves.[7]

Beth-el members provide relief services—such as providing people in need with food, clothes, and household supplies—from the renovated first floor of the storefront. The second floor was turned into classrooms for teaching computer literacy, software, financial management, parenting, and so forth. On the third floor, elder care is provided during the day. There are also community social activities. Toward the end of the day, they run after-school care for children and provide homework help. Child care is desperately needed because most of the parents in that community must have two or three jobs in order to survive. The church also holds its worship services in this building, and some people whom it helps during the week come.

The church runs a health-food store in another storefront next door. This store provides vouchers that give large discounts for the people who attend their healthy-eating classes, so they can afford the products they learn about in class.

Beth-el is involved with prison ministries. They work with the prisoners' families—mentoring them on how to survive and teaching them job skills. When the prisoners are released, the church members also teach them job skills.

Three years after Beth-el was established, the local government affirmed them for their good work and assigned three caseworkers to work with Beth-el. The church is mingling and working *with* their community.

Portland Adventist Community Services

Portland Adventist Community Services (PACS) is located in Portland, Oregon, U.S.A., and is part of a worldwide network of Adventist Community Service centers that are either in an Adventist church or in a separate building. There are no two Adventist Community Service centers alike, for their services are based on the needs of the neighborhoods they serve.

The prayer of the PACS staff for those whom they serve aligns with that of the apostle John: "I pray that you may enjoy good health and that all may go well with you, even as your soul is getting along well" (3 John 2). Their services include a top-notch thrift store, an affordable medical clinic for low-income families, a food pantry in a free-choice grocery store format, and a mobile food pantry for underserved neighborhoods; a dental clinic is also being planned.

Originally, PACS distributed food the conventional way: assembling bags of food and giving clothes and household supplies to those who came to the center. The recipients had no choice in what food they received. Rhonda Whitney, the former director, and her staff observed that many of those who came to the center for assistance did not appear to be happy about their visit at the center, especially when they came for food. Rhonda and the PACS staff prayed about this and decided hesitantly to set up a free-choice food distribution system in a grocery-store format. The staff moved reluctantly to this setup because it would be a lot of work and would be unfamiliar to them. "We wanted people who came to PACS for assistance to leave feeling like they have been with Jesus while here," Rhonda said.

The staff set up the grocery-store format and watched to see what would happen. The recipients were happy and their dignity was preserved when they could make their own choices. The staff enthusiastically decided to never go back to the former system of food distribution.

PACS cares about the good of those whom they serve, even if it means drastic changes to their previous methods.

Not a thread of selfishness

"The Saviour mingled with men as one who desired *their good.*"[8] This is the right motive for mingling. The reason we mingle is as important as the mingling. It must be for the good of others, not merely for what good we will get out of it, as demonstrated by the sample churches above.

"His [Jesus'] was the medical missionary work that He asks His people to do today. Humble, gracious, tenderhearted, pitiful [full of pity], He went about doing good, feeding the hungry, lifting up the bowed down, comforting the sorrowing. None who came to Him for aid went away unrelieved. *Not a thread of selfishness* was woven into the pattern He has left for His children to follow. He lived the life that He would have all live who believe on Him."[9]

Are you following "the pattern"?

> When your church does evangelistic meetings, plan community services not only to attract people to the meetings, but to serve your community *continuously*—meetings or no meetings—because you desire their good and you care!

1. Ellen G. White, *The Desire of Ages,* 504.

2. Ellen G. White, "Ellen G. White Comments," in *The Seventh-day Adventist Bible Commentary,* 5:1140; emphasis added.

3. Nelson, *Pursuing the Passion of Jesus,* 57.

4. Ibid., adapted.

5. The same attitude flowed from inside the early church into the lives of the pagans on the outside, causing the early Christian church to take over the Roman Empire. Historian Rodney Stark concludes that early Christian church members cared not only for their own poor, but for the pagan poor—a major reason the early church grew so rapidly. Stark, *Cities of God* (New York: HarperCollins Publishers, 2006), 31.

6. Ellen G. White, *Patriarchs and Prophets* (Mountain View, CA: Pacific Press® Publishing Association, 1958), 140.

7. Adapted from a definition of "church" by Wayne Krause.

8. White, *The Ministry of Healing,* 143; emphasis added.

9. White, *Welfare Ministry,* 116; emphasis added.

CHAPTER 8

Jesus Showed Sympathy

Nameless woman

She slunk along the dusty road toward the Sea of Galilee. Rumor had it that Jesus of Nazareth was coming back to Capernaum from Decapolis. *What would He be doing there? That's Gentile country,* she thought. Refocusing on her objective, the nameless woman shuffled along, keeping her legs together to hold her wrappings in place. Jesus always had a crowd with Him, and He always took the same road into town from the fishing village. In frightened anticipation, she thought through her plan.

The nameless woman heard that Jesus' teaching was compelling; many were not only healed, but their whole lives were changed. Because of this, Nameless determined to go out and find Jesus—an act that broke her social restrictions. For twelve years, she had suffered with bleeding. At first, she thought it was a simple irregularity of her monthly cycle, but it did not stop—twelve years of staying home in her family compound. Jewish laws forbade her from going to public places, such as the marketplace, social gatherings, and even to the synagogue. Her intimate relationship with her husband was ruined; her social circle had all but collapsed; and she was nobody. She knew that Jesus could not touch her without becoming unclean Himself. But she also knew that Jesus was so great a healer that entire villages were made well by His presence; maybe a simple touch of His garment would be enough.

The crowd enveloped Jesus. Nameless knew He was in there some-where, but how to reach Him without drawing attention to herself was still a conundrum. As she plotted the angle in which she could enter the crowd inconspicuously, the crowd began to split open in deference to Jairus, the synagogue ruler. She knew who he was. Everybody knew who he was. Why would he be . . . ?

Jairus fell at Jesus' feet, pleading for Jesus to come and place His hands on his dying daughter. Jesus agreed, and the crowd accelerated toward Jairus's house. *Oh, Lord, what shall I do?* Nameless thought. Shuffling through the fast-moving mass of humanity, desperate to accomplish her purpose, Nameless dropped to her knees and quickly reached out to touch Jesus' garment anonymously. She could barely see through the dust being kicked up around her face. She had angled her-self in such a way so Jesus would step right by her. All she needed was to endure the jostling of hasty feet around her. Hope escalated in her heart as she identified the feet of the Savior, and, there—she had done it! She touched the hem of Jesus' garment! What was that feeling? Suddenly, there was a trembling deep inside her. A feeling of wellness engulfed her. Nameless sighed with peace as jostling feet knocked her about.

"Who touched Me?" asked Jesus. Those around Jesus laughed, knowing that the crowd was pressing Him on all sides. But Jesus stopped, and the people stepped back. Sudden terror struck Nameless. This was not supposed to happen! And there was Jesus looking at *her*. There was no sign of irritation on His face. The interruption didn't seem to faze Him. The hurried pace of the noisy multitude following Jairus toward his home was suddenly halted. Silence enveloped everyone. Nameless expected that Jesus and the crowd would move on quickly to answer Jairus's emergency, but Jesus didn't move. Feeling conspicuous, she began to explain to Jesus why she had come and what she had done (Luke 8:47). Jesus' eyes invited her confidence; she knew that He under-stood her plight. Somehow she felt that she could talk to Him without fear or hurry. Jesus made no move to leave in spite of the nervous agita-tion of Jairus and the multitude.

In the distance, there was murmuring, and Jairus began to sob. Without breaking His attention from Nameless, Jesus gently said, "Daughter, your faith has healed you. Go in peace and be freed from your suffering" (Mark 5:34).

Jesus Showed Sympathy

Jairus was heartbroken; a messenger had arrived with the news of his daughter's death. With the same tenderness offered to Nameless, Jesus turned to Jairus and whispered soothingly, "Don't be afraid; just believe, and she will be healed" (Luke 8:50). As Nameless watched the departing crowd, she thought to herself, *He stopped for me even though a more important person was waiting. He listened to me and made me feel like the most important person in the world to Him. He cared enough to stop, listen, and sympathize with my plight. Wow!*

Showing sympathy

Jesus did not only define the word *sympathy;* He *showed* it! Showing sympathy was the perspective from which He treated people. The words related to *sympathy,* such as *pity* and *empathy,* are connected to the word *compassion.* Dacher Keltner states that the basic tools of compassion are "an appreciation of others' suffering and a desire to remedy that suffering."[1] Jesus demonstrated that concept when He fed the five thousand men, plus women and children: "When Jesus landed and saw a large crowd, he had compassion on them *and* healed their sick" (Matthew 14:14; emphasis added).

Jesus' followers will move beyond the emotional feeling of sympathy to *showing* sympathy. *Eleēmosunē,* another Greek word, means "to *show* sympathy." This use of the word refers to an act in contrast to mere emotion. It leads to benevolent activity and is often associated with helping through the giving of alms. In Acts 9:36, we meet Tabitha (Dorcas), who was always doing good and *showing sympathy* (*eleēmosunē*) to the poor.

When Dorcas looked around her, there were many hurting people. She did not see them as problems, but, like Jesus, she saw their human faces and immediately began to respond. Below are stories of Seventh-day Adventist Church members who go beyond seeing people and their struggles as problems that are "so sad" or "too bad."

Showing sympathy to brokenhearted and oppressed children

The members of the Newport, Tennessee, Seventh-day Adventist Church are showing sympathy for and bringing comfort and emotional healing to traumatized foster children.[2] In partnership with churches of other denominations in the region, Newport church member Carole

Colburn directs an outreach ministry called It's My Very Own (IMVO). Approximately fifteen women from these various churches join Newport members at the Newport Seventh-day Adventist Church on Monday mornings and produce "Bags of Love" for the IMVO ministry. In addition to volunteers, the partner churches provide financial support.

The women lovingly make beautiful quilts and large colorful cloth bags, in which they put the quilts, along with toys, stuffed animals, personal care items (comb, hairbrush, toothbrush, toothpaste, and such), books, and so forth. These are delivered to the child protective services departments in the neighboring ten counties. When children are removed from abusive homes, they generally cannot take anything with them to foster homes. When they receive a Bag of Love, they now have something they can call their very own. On each quilt, there is a tag that reads, " 'It's My Very Own' Bags of Love—Made for you by the hearts and hands of the people of your community. Sponsored by the Seventh-day Adventist Church."

At the time of this writing, the women have made and distributed more than sixteen hundred quilts and bags. Because of confidentiality issues, they may never know most of the reactions to their loving work. A few responses have reached their ears: "These bags make such a difference to the kids. They come into our office scared to death. But the minute they are given these bags, it's like Christmas." "Even the teenage boys come into the office with their quilts thrown over their shoulders." A foster parent telephoned Carole Colburn and said, "I'm so glad to reach someone who is involved in making these quilts and bags. Just recently we were given two children to keep—a boy age six and a girl age nine. When they came to us they brought these bags with them. And now they will hardly let the quilts out of their sight; even though the weather is warm, they insist on sleeping with the quilts. And the little boy is apparently really missing his father—because he calls his teddy bear 'Daddy' and sleeps with him every night."

Again and again this foster mother repeated, "You don't know what a difference these bags make to these children. What a difference, what a difference! Now they have something they can call their very own."

Some of the women from the community who are involved in IMVO are attending the Newport church regularly. As they have shown mercy to the oppressed in their community, the Lord's mercy has reached them too. Carole rejoices that the Lord impressed Barbara Neher in Kentucky, U.S.A., to start the IMVO work several years ago and to share it through ASI.[3] Other churches have started similar IMVO groups.

In Isaiah 61, the prophet Isaiah describes that the mission of the Messiah is to "bind up the brokenhearted, . . . to comfort all who mourn, and provide for those who grieve," providing "a garment of praise instead of a spirit of despair" (verses 1–3). Followers of Jesus do the same.

Showing sympathy to AIDS victims

The nameless woman was considered unclean; she touched Jesus (Matthew 9:20). Lepers were considered unclean; Jesus touched them (Matthew 8:3). In modern times, AIDS carries a certain stigma of uncleanness. AIDS victims and their families are in dire need of sympathy that is followed up with compassionate care. Drs. Oscar and Eugenia Giordano see AIDS not merely as a serious social problem. Instead, they see the faces of the victims of this deadly disease as they direct Adventist AIDS International Ministry (AAIM). AAIM is a special ministry of the Seventh-day Adventist Church that helps to mobilize the Adventist network of churches and institutions in response to the HIV/AIDS epidemic. AAIM started in 2004 and serves those affected and infected by AIDS in several African countries.

Everything is done through the churches, which are known as centers of hope and healing. For example, there are HIV/AIDS education programs, support for grandmothers (grandmothers' clubs), feeding programs, home-based care, income-generating activities, sewing workshops and education for other skills, community development activities, gardens, care for orphans, and clothing and shoe distributions. In addition, the churches run special educational programs for youth that address resilience and prevention of risky behaviors.

Showing sympathy to prisoners—prison ministries in Panama

"I was in prison and you came to visit me" (Matthew 25:36). Seventh-day Adventist Church members all over the world have responded to Jesus' words regarding prison ministries. The following is one of many examples.

In Panama, Dona Rosa Tamburrelli's community presented her with a plaque honoring her for the positive impact she has made on female prisoners' lives and for her efforts in reintegrating these women back into society. Every year Dona Rosa conducts an evangelistic reaping meeting within the walls of the rehabilitation center. So far, approximately 450 prisoners have given their lives to God during these meetings. Additionally, every week she provides toiletries, medicine, and other needed items to the prisoners.[4] Daily, Dona Rosa follows this counsel from Ellen White: "If we would humble ourselves before God, and be kind and courteous and tenderhearted and pitiful [showing pity], there would be one hundred conversions to the truth where now there is only one."[5]

Showing sympathy to the sick and discouraged

Vernon Luthas, an anesthesiologist at Kettering Medical Center in Kettering, Ohio, U.S.A., showed sympathy by visiting and praying with his patients the night before surgery. Once he met an older woman who told him, "I've waited a long time to tell you this, but I wanted you to know that the prayer you offered for me on the day before my operation—it was that prayer that made me a Christian. Today I am a Seventh-day Adventist, and I just wanted you to know that." The surgery had occurred twenty-five years earlier. Adventist hospitals, clinics, and dispensaries worldwide—and their medical staff, chaplains, and other personnel—are channels for the sympathy and love of Jesus Christ.[6]

Showing sympathy to the grieving

Grief is natural and normal mental distress over the loss of anyone or anything that means a lot to you. The grieving process is feeling great sorrow and pain over this loss and is an opportunity to mourn appropriately and move toward healing. Therese A. Rando describes grief as "the process that allows us to let go of that which was and be ready for that which is to come."[7]

Job lost his family (except for his wife), his belongings, and his health within a short time. What he needed was heartfelt sympathy and encouragement as he grieved. What he got was the "sympathy" of three "friends" who held good intentions but got it all wrong (Job 2:11).

Jesus Showed Sympathy

We need to know how to comfort the sorrowful in a healing way. If we are not careful, we can do more harm than good. It is important to understand what emotional responses people may have when grieving so that we can show sympathy in a way that will help, not hurt, them.

Many descriptions of the grieving process have been offered to help with understanding it, with different names for the elements of grieving. One major example is found in Dr. Elisabeth Kübler-Ross's 1969 book *On Death and Dying,* where she introduced the five stages of grief (also known as the Kübler-Ross model). Dr. Kübler-Ross's five stages are guideposts about normal reactions to deep loss and are intended to help those experiencing loss to identify what they may be feeling. Knowing the five stages can also help friends and family of the grieving person to better understand the grief process.

The five stages are (1) denial, (2) anger, (3) bargaining (willing to do anything to avoid or undo the loss), (4) depression, and (5) acceptance. Many sufferers and those who are endeavoring to comfort them have found the Kübler-Ross model useful in a variety of loss situations, such as in grieving a death, a divorce, a break-up, substance abuse, the loss of a job, and so forth.

The stages of grief are five common reactions, but not necessarily a required formula. People respond to loss in their own unique ways, and not everyone goes through all five stages or in a specific order. Stages can overlap or occur together, or a person might jump back and forth among the stages. Grieving is a personal process that does not have a time limit. Grievers spend varied amounts of time working through the steps and at different levels of intensity. Sometimes emotions are like a roller coaster—all over the place. A person may grieve for the past, present, and future. There is no finish line in grieving. Acceptance is not final; it shifts and changes.

Understanding grieving can lead us to show *true* sympathy. Here are some additional suggestions:

- Be present—in the moment. Depending on the circumstances, it may be good to show up at the grievers' residence and invite them to go with you on your errands, for example.
- It is important to listen to what the grieving ones wish to tell us about their needs. Let them talk about anything that's on their

minds. Do not evaluate and judge (Matthew 7:1).

- Showing sympathy is not just an intellectual exercise. There is a deep emotional and physical side. "Jesus wept" and was "deeply moved" because Lazarus had died (John 11:35, 38).
- It is never wrong to grieve. Do not say, "You shouldn't feel that way. It will be OK. Have faith in God."
- Be careful how you show empathy (identifying with the feelings or situation of another person). Do not "one up" those who are grieving (e.g., "I'm so sorry about your grandmother's passing. Last year, my grandmother *and* my mother passed away around the same time.").
- Consider taking a course that prepares you to provide crisis care for emotional and spiritual support for those walking the path of grief.[8]
- Pastors should pastor their communities, not only their church members. Crisis care preparation helps with this.
- Maintain balance and self-care in your life as you identify with and show compassion to others.
- Make a memory book of a loved one who died and give it to the grieving spouse or family as a gift.
- Read the local newspaper, noting bereavements and local tragedies. Follow up with sympathy cards and other tangible love-motivated expressions of sympathy from your church.
- Many Seventh-day Adventist churches worldwide have grief recovery groups for their own faith community and their neighborhoods or communities. There are various prepared resources that churches can use in this ministry, such as GriefShare.[9]
- Know your limits. Refer people to professional counselors when necessary.

Show all sides of sympathy

We have portrayed sympathy in this chapter mostly in connection with sad situations. An additional definition of *sympathy* is "harmony of or agreement in feeling, as between persons."[10] Someone has said, "Shared joy is double joy, and shared sorrow is half sorrow." The Bible says, "Rejoice with them that do rejoice, and weep with them that weep" (Romans 12:15, KJV). Therefore, showing sympathy could also mean rejoicing with those who rejoice.

"There is need of coming close to the people by personal effort. . . . *We are to weep with those that weep, and rejoice with those that rejoice.* Accompanied by the power of persuasion, the power of prayer, the power of the love of God, this work will not, cannot, be without fruit."[11]

There is suffering (and rejoicing) all around us, among the poor, middle class, and rich. Go to someone and *show* sympathy after praying for divine help to guide you, choose your words for you, and let you know when silence is best.[12] Then go, and be in the sad or happy moment with that person.

1. Dacher Keltner, "The Compassionate Instinct," *Greater Good,* March 1, 2004, accessed October 1, 2015, http://greatergood.berkeley.edu/article/item/the_compassionate_instinct.

2. This section is adapted from May-Ellen Colón, "Where Is God Already Active in Your Community and How Can You Join Him?" *Elder's Digest,* October–December 2014, 20, 21.

3. ASI is Adventist-laymen's Services & Industries. The ASI Web site states, "Adventist-laymen's Services & Industries is a cooperative network of lay individuals, professionals, business owners, and ministries who collectively support the global mission of the Seventh-day Adventist Church." See www.asiministries.org.

4. Adapted from "Prison Ministries: Moldova and Panama," *Adventist World,* June 2011, 19, accessed October 1, 2015, http://issuu.com/adventistworldmagazine/docs/aw1006_jun11 _english.

5. Ellen G. White, *Testimonies for the Church,* 9:189.

6. This story is from *Kettering Medical Center: Fifty Years of Caring and Innovation, Heritage Edition* (2014), DVD.

7. Therese A. Rando, *Grief, Dying, and Death: Clinical Interventions for Caregivers* (Champaign, IL: Research Press, 1984), 17. Another of Therese Rando's books is *How to Go on Living When Someone You Love Dies* (New York: Bantam Books, 1991).

8. The North American Division's Adventist Community Services Crisis Care curriculum educates and equips volunteers to provide emotional and spiritual care for traumatized survivors of disasters and other critical incidents. For more information, go to http://www .communityservices.org/.

9. For information on Grief Share, go to www.griefshare.org/.

10. *Dictionary.com,* s.v. "sympathy," accessed August 18, 2015, http://dictionary.reference .com/browse/sympathy?s=t.

11. White, *The Ministry of Healing,* 143; emphasis added.

12. See Ellen G. White, *Messages to Young People* (Nashville: Southern Publishing Association, 1930), 90.

CHAPTER

Jesus Ministered to Their Needs

"Failed" mission trip a *big* success

A man in a clown suit plops into a hair-salon chair in a small Australian town.[1] "I'm here for a perm," he announces. The folks in the shop all laugh, and someone shouts, "StormCo is back!" They proceed to give a warm welcome to Crunchy the Clown—actually Chrys Martin, a StormCo team leader and member of the Avondale Memorial Seventh-day Adventist Church in Cooranbong, New South Wales, Australia.

StormCo, a mission concept born in Australia, which stands for Service to Others Really Matters Company, is the result of a planned mission trip that fell through at the last minute. More than twenty years ago, Jerry Unser was urgently trying to find something adventurous for the team of disappointed young people who were ready to go on their long-awaited (now canceled) mission trip. Unser called pastors in the region until he found one who invited the group to stay at his church while they looked around the small town to find something useful to do.

The group ended up visiting schools and local churches, holding cooking classes, and hanging out with indigenous community members. When the group returned home, they excitedly looked forward to doing it again.

Now the program has become a widespread international movement. Generally, teams of fifteen to twenty youth are sent out on seven- to

81

ten-day mission trips each year. What is the secret of StormCo's success? It's StormCo's approach to the community: (1) The teams endeavor to create strong relationships built on trust, so they return to the same community year after year. (2) *Instead of arriving in the neighborhood with a predetermined program, they go with no agenda, and ask town leaders what their needs are and what ways StormCo can engage with the community.*

Such community assessment has led the different teams to do many types of adventurous and unexpected activities and programs, depending on the counsel of community leaders. For example, in one town a team runs a Kids' Club, with Christian songs, puppet shows, Bible story plays, crafts, and games.

The teams have noticed changes for the better in many kids from rough environments who have attended a Kids' Club. One mother was thrilled that her two girls learned about Jesus, and now they sing songs about Jesus at home. Another StormCo team was asked to take over the local radio station in their target area, run the equipment, make announcements, report news, and play Christian music. The station managers really appreciate their help. In the afternoon, this team takes on various community service jobs, such as painting projects, repairing buildings, and cleaning up church yards. They even paid to replace a leaky water tank at a Catholic church. Another team facilitated youth nights with partner-type games and bonfires with testimonies about what God has done for them.

StormCo leaders concluded that the StormCo method of meeting with town leaders and asking them about their needs, followed by asking how the team of young people could help, was the turnaround in the attitude of many communities toward StormCo and the Seventh-day Adventist Church. StormCo prepares the way to share with many neighborhoods the love of Christ and His salvation.

StormCo reflects the attitude Christ had while He was on earth, for Christ's agenda was to mingle with people, *discover* their needs, and then meet those needs. He was open to whoever and whatever came His way. Many of His needs-meeting experiences came out of a series of interruptions. Regardless of what He was going through, even when mourning for a loved one (John the Baptist), Jesus unselfishly met the needs of those around Him.

Foiled getaway a *big* blessing

The amazing story of Jesus feeding five thousand hungry men, plus women and children, is recorded in all four of the Gospels (Matthew 14:13–21; Mark 6:30–44; Luke 9:10–17; John 6:1–14). Imagine that you were present that day. Not long before, John the Baptist's disciples had arrived with tragic news. Breathlessly, they recounted how Herod's niece and his sister-in-law Herodias had duped Herod into beheading John the Baptist. Deeply moved by the loss of His relative[2] and forerunner, John, Jesus calls His disciples to retreat by boat to the north side of Galilee near the town of Bethsaida. With such sad news, the group longed to move away from the crowds to reflect and pray.

However, word had spread that Jesus and His disciples were heading to Bethsaida. The multitude managed to meet the mourning travelers near the shores of Bethsaida's fishing village and seemed as eager to be with Jesus as He and His disciples longed for peace and quiet. Arriving in groups, the people's faces shone with joy when they saw the Master, knowing He would heal their sick and longing for more knowledge of the kingdom. Once again, Jesus had a big crowd. Why? He was meeting needs.

Evening approached, and the multitude of listeners showed no inclination to leave. Knowing this impromptu meeting would need to come to an end soon if the crowd were to be afforded the opportunity to find food in town, the disciples spoke with Jesus. In response, Jesus must have smiled (and maybe winked) as He challenged His disciples to find a way to feed them. The need was obvious; the means were meager. All that was available was a boy's small lunch (John 6:8, 9).

Jesus' disciples started by identifying what was available. With inadequate resources, Jesus miraculously and abundantly met the multitude's need, and a surplus of twelve baskets of bread and fish were left. The blow of sadness that had hit Jesus and His disciples over the tragic loss of John the Baptist was softened. And an interrupted quest for retreat turned into a blessing for thousands. What a God! (See Ephesians 3:20, 21.)

Practical guidelines today for implementing Christ's approach to meeting needs

The natural progression of Jesus' ministry was mingling with people, discovering their needs, and responding to those needs. Too many churches today think they already know the needs of the people in their communities or neighborhoods—without mingling with them. Even though churches may provide social services and do good works for the community, Robert Linthicum calls this attitude a "fatal flaw" in ministry.[3] Doing programs *before* consulting the people is like "fire, aim, ready" instead of "ready, aim, fire"! Linthicum labels this type of church response to community needs "the church *to* the city [community]."[4]

Rather than trying to break into our community or neighborhood to share Jesus, we must first put forth the effort of talking to the people about their needs. This lets them know we care, and it informs us on how we can serve in ways that will be appreciated. We will also make new friends and prepare them to feel a need they may not know they have: Jesus! We will continue to address this issue in chapter 11. In addition to searching for needs, a critical part is also discovering the strengths in the community on which your church can build and partner.

To effectively discover and respond to the needs and strengths of your community, your church must commit itself to an intentional *process*. To get you started, here are effective steps that various churches have used:

1. Your church needs to ask itself, *How* can *we* help? What do we have to offer our community? To discover this, have each church member fill out a form that indicates their areas of expertise and experience and the times during the week they are available to serve. After Jesus told the disciples to give the huge crowd something to eat, He asked His disciples, "What do *you* have?" (see Mark 6:38). He asks us that today: What is the "little boy's lunch" your church can use to help meet your community's needs?

2. Next appoint a team of four to six people to systematically study your church's community and mobilize all departments and members toward responding to the discovered needs. Some

churches call this team the social action leadership team (SALT).[5]

3. Narrow down your church's ministry territory. Get a map of your region, and draw a circle on it that represents the radius of your territory, using your church or Community Services center as the center point. Monte Sahlin recommends a radius of three miles (five kilometers) out in an urban setting (if the population is really dense, perhaps twenty blocks is enough to start with); nine miles (fifteen kilometers) out in a suburban area; and approximately fifteen miles (twenty-four kilometers) out if your church is in a small town or rural area.

4. Once you have determined the territory, tell your group to symbolically put on their "ministry glasses" and take a walk or drive through it in groups of two to get a visual survey. Cover every street, or at least follow an intentional grid pattern, doing every third or fifth street. Take notes, listing ministry ideas you saw through your "ministry glasses." In rural areas, a driver and a note-taker will drive through random samples of your entire territory. After a couple of hours, have a debriefing session with all the groups. Share your observations and what this means to your ministry goals. Jesus walked around His ministry territory to get the feel of His surroundings and the needs of the people; the apostle Paul also understood this concept. Before he spoke in Athens at Mars' Hill (the Areopagus), Paul took a walking survey around the neighborhood (Acts 17:22, 23).

5. Another important step in preparing to serve in your territory is obtaining demographic information for the area from libraries, government census reports, or various Web sites. This will answer questions about the number of people, the median age, ethnicities, religions, economic situations, education levels, and so forth. In Jesus' day, governments took a census for the purpose of taxation (Luke 2:1–3), which might have provided this type of information. Being God, Jesus did not need to do this step in the same way we do. His omniscience enabled Him to already know about the personal lives of those He served (e.g., John 1:47–49).

6. After practicing ahead of time, the SALT should interview (two by two is best) a balanced sample of the main community leaders, such as those in business, education, government, health and

social services, media, and religion. (Aim for interviewing at least twelve to eighteen community leaders.) Ask the leaders such questions as, (1) What are the strengths in this community? (2) What are some of the most important needs in this community? (3) What could my church or organization do to help meet some of these needs? (4) What do you know about my church? (It is helpful to know how your church is coming across in the community and, thus, be motivated to improve this image.) The team members should take notes and organize the responses under each question; note the key themes that surface.[6]

After following these first six steps to assess your community, you may discover ministry opportunities you did not expect—needs among the rich as well as the poor. "Much is said concerning our duty to the neglected poor; should not some attention be given to the neglected rich? . . . Many among the rich are soul-burdened."[7] Another ministry opportunity may include people with special needs, such as the deaf, blind, and people with other disabilities. Your church may want to look into setting up signing for the deaf for church services and other meetings, or helping the blind connect with resources that are designed for them, such as those offered by Christian Record Services for the Blind.[8]

7. Make a report that includes the findings from the community assessment steps, which will contribute to a strategic ministry plan for your church. This ministry plan is to be based on scriptural principles, the input from your community, and the ministry vision of your church members.

Some leaders use an "appreciative inquiry" (AI) to capture the ministry vision of church members.[9] To implement this, invite church members to attend a business meeting for the sole purpose of remembering life-giving experiences in Adventist churches in the members' past and present; then brainstorm positive ideas for improvements they would like to see. Tell them not to focus on problems but to focus instead on dreams they have for their church—dreams in which only God's intervention will guarantee success! Write down their positive ideas in the meeting and categorize them into themes. Create a five-year plan. Each year focus on a different aspect of the five-year plan. Produce a strategic ministry plan based on all this input.

After approval from a church business meeting and the church board, implement the ministry plan. The success of a strategic plan is its implementation! Every year the plan should be evaluated in a business meeting and adjusted accordingly. During the fifth year, get your church members together for another brainstorming session and work toward a vision for the next five years. Continue the annual plan review until Jesus' second coming.

This process of positioning your church to meet the needs in your community demonstrates that in order to effectively serve the community, the strategy "must be locally invented and developed!"[10]

Zwelitsha Seventh-day Adventist Church showers public primary school with gifts

The Zwelitsha Seventh-day Adventist Church in South Africa discovered a need in its community and tapped into community resources to help meet that need. Together with community partners, the church supplied twenty-four needy pupils in Ngqika Junior Primary School with school uniforms. Each of these pupils received a full winter uniform, consisting of a pair of school shoes, a long-sleeve shirt, a pair of school socks, a school tie, a school sweater, and a pair of gray trousers or a school dress.

The Adventist Women's Ministries and Adventist Men clubs in the Zwelitsha church contributed much to provide funds for the school clothing. Additionally, several businesses and medical practices in King William's Town and Zwelitsha supported the church in this compassionate endeavor. The ceremony for handing over the uniforms to the twenty-four pupils was a high day for the residents of Zwelitsha. Members of the local governement were also present during the ceremony. The ward councillor was also present.

During the ceremony, a government official pledged to support students who were identified as needy but could not be helped by the Adventist church because of the church's limited resources. He also mentioned noting some infrastructure challenges that seemed to warrant immediate attention and that he would send a delegation to make a formal inquiry and recommendations for the possible intervention of the Department of Education and its strategic partners.

The keynote address by the official was very encouraging to the parents of the beneficiaries. He encouraged these parents to continue with their tireless efforts to provide for their children's learning needs within their limited resources and in spite of the unemployment experienced by most of the parents. He visualized a beautiful scene of many parents across the economic spectrum taking their children to junior primary schools every day. He also encouraged ordinary South Africans such as the Zwelitsha Seventh-day Adventist Church members to continue doing the little they can to contribute to the educational needs of the children, as education is considered the best tool to break the cycle of poverty.

This story is a splendid example of what can happen when various church departments partner to reach out and when the church partners with segments of its community and neighborhood, such as businesses, health care, and government, to meet needs and build on community strengths and resources.

> Make plans to assess your community; follow up with a definite plan to meet the discovered needs; and build on the discovered strengths and resources.[11]

---

1. This section is adapted from Sandra Blackmer, "From Australia's Outback: Service to Others Really Matters," *Adventist World*, February 2014, 16–20.

2. See Luke 1:36.

3. Robert C. Linthicum, *Empowering the Poor: Community Organizing Among the City's "Rag, Tag and Bobtail"* (Monrovia, CA: MARC, 1991), 22.

4. Ibid. Linthicum presents two additional approaches to meeting community needs: the church in the community (the church ignores the needs in its neighborhood as it focuses on preserving its own life—like being in a fortress); and the church with the community (the church joins in the community's struggle to determine for itself what kind of community it wants, and it partners with the community to make it happen). Ibid., 21–24.

5. Other language groups might want to invent another related acronym or initialism.

6. For more information on community assessment, see Monte Sahlin, *Understanding Your Community* (Milton-Freewater, OR: Center for Creative Ministry, 2001).

7. Ellen G. White, *The Ministry of Healing*, 210.

8. For more information on resources for the blind, go to the Web site for Christian Record

Jesus Ministered to Their Needs

Services for the Blind: http://www.christianrecord.org/.

9. AI is a process of searching for the best in people and their organizations. Here are three AI items to consider for your church: (1) Think back to the most energizing and life-giving experiences you have ever had in relation to the Seventh-day Adventist Church. What was going on in your life and in the church? (2) What do you appreciate most about your church, and how does it contribute to your spiritual walk? (3) What improvements would you like to see? (No negatives.)

10. Sahlin, *Understanding Your Community.*

11. For more information about building on community strengths and resources, see chapter 10.

CHAPTER

Jesus Won Their Confidence

True success pathway

In our journey toward understanding Christ's method of reaching people, we have examined Christ's passion for socializing (mingling), sympathizing, and serving (ministering to people's needs). It is obvious that this progression leads to the winning of *confidence*. Built into the word *confidence* is the concept of trust (faith). The first three steps of Christ's ministry method can be arranged as a formula: socializing + sympathizing + serving = confidence.

Pagan military officer shows confidence in Jesus

Jesus attracted people. Though His discourse on the side of the mountain was intended as a training session for His disciples, the multitudes could not stay away (Matthew 5–7). Jesus' presence, His compassion, and His service were cherished; and people felt attracted to His authenticity in contrast to the hypocritical and ostentatious demeanor of the religious leaders of the day.

As Jesus entered the city of Capernaum, a Roman soldier of high rank approached Him (Matthew 8:5–13); this centurion had observed all that Jesus was doing for individuals wherever He went. When his servant fell ill, the centurion became deeply concerned. His servant lay paralyzed and near death; the only remedy the centurion could see was to have Jesus heal his servant. He could not resist his attraction to Jesus, whom he trusted to meet his need. Jesus willingly offered to go to the centurion's home to heal the servant, but the centurion simply trusted that Jesus could simply say the word and the healing would occur. Perhaps this Roman soldier knew enough Jewish tradition to realize that Jews (and therefore, in his mind, maybe Jesus) did not wish to become defiled by entering a Gentile home. Perhaps he simply wanted to confirm publicly his confidence in Jesus. Either way, to all who witnessed the scene, it was clear that Jesus held the centurion's confidence.

Authentic Christians who mingle with those around them, sympathize with the needs of others, and unselfishly serve will earn the confidence of those around them. Christ shines through His followers, displaying an authenticity that attracts all who otherwise would turn away. A popular quote, often attributed to Mahatma Gandhi, goes, "I like your Christ; I do not like your Christians. Your Christians are so unlike your Christ." On behalf of Christ, have we earned the confidence of those around us—or does Gandhi's statement apply to us?

Non-Christian Chinese government officer shows confidence in followers of Jesus

In China, a Christian pastor and his wife rented an apartment near a university campus. They often invited students, both Christians and non-Christians, to their apartment. Sometimes they shared Bible stories, sometimes Christian songs, and sometimes they just invited them for dinner. During Chinese festivals, most students went home to their families, but some students lived far away and chose to stay on campus. The pastor and his wife prepared lots of delicious food and invited to their home those students who stayed on campus so they would not feel so lonely. This university ministry lasted many years, until the pastor and his wife left the area to pursue missionary work elsewhere.

Years later, a natural disaster erupted in Southwest China. The same pastor led a Christian medical team to that region to do some rescue work as well as spread the gospel to the people in that area. Normally, the local government would refuse Christian groups for political reasons. However, this time, to their surprise, the team led by the pastor entered that region without any trouble. They heard that there was a certain local county governor who approved the entry of their team, saying, "Christians are good guys. Let them do anything they want."

Later, the pastor met the governor and asked him why he would let a Christian team enter his county. With a smile, the governor replied, "Oh, I ate many meals in a Christian's house years ago when I was a poor university student. I still remember the delicious food on special festivals." Amazed by this, the pastor praised God that this man had been one of his university fellowship guests so many years ago.

Social capital worth more than money

The Chinese pastor had earned social capital. Winning confidence is connected with the concept of social capital; it is all about building relationships. Just as when one makes investments in a bank account, so each investment in a relationship in the community will cause your social capital to grow. However, social capital is worth more than money; more can be accomplished with social capital than without it.

Social capital is particularly important for God's church in these end times, because a church often operates on limited means and is largely a volunteer group. When your church builds up a social capital "account," this will be a major asset to help your church attain significant goals that it could not achieve alone. For your church to tap into its social capital account, it is wise to understand the social capital to which you have access in your neighborhood. What is in your social capital account? In other words, what potential partners are there to work with your church in accomplishing positive change? After all, you don't need to invent all of your outreach projects and activities!

Before you can access the benefits of the social capital that potentially exists within your neighborhood, your church needs a clear picture of its relationships, networks, and connections. James Krile, in *The Community Leadership Handbook,* suggests that a good first step is to create a "social capital map."[1]

One way to create a social capital map is to make a chart with columns labeled as follows (see the example below): (1) at the top of the first column, write "Organizations/Individuals" and list those in the community with whom your church has a relationship. Allow space for names, e-mail addresses, and phone numbers in the list. (2) Label the second column "Strength of Tie." Write "Strong" or "Weak" to indicate your guess about the strength of your tie with each listed organization or individual. (3) Write "Resources" at the top of the third column, and list the specific resources each group or individual might provide in your specific project or goal to meet community needs. (4) Write "Next Steps" at the top of the last column.

Social capital map:
Possible community partners

ORGANIZATIONS/ INDIVIDUALS (Include contact person's name, email address, and phone number)	STRENGTH OF TIE Strong/Weak	RESOURCES	NEXT STEPS
Public (government):			
Private (businesses/organizations):			
Nonprofit/Humanitarian:			
Other Religions:			

When filling out column 1, remember to strive for whole community involvement in your planning. It is important to have a wide range of relationships in order to implement significant community service projects. List individuals and organizations from all four sectors in your community: public, private, nonprofit, and other religions.

In column 2 (Strength of Tie), the concepts of strong and weak ties with potential community partners refer to the degrees of trust in each other (honesty, integrity, reliability), reciprocity (mutual benefit from the relationship), and durability (lasting over time through stress and changing circumstances).[2]

What are your next steps?

Follow through on your list. Take intentional steps to nurture and enhance your relationships with the listed organizations and individuals. Strengthen the ties and thus increase their confidence in your church. Not only should you desire social capital for your church, but you will also want to be social capital for organizations and individuals in your neighborhood that are compatible with your mission. Such an attitude will go far in winning the trust and confidence of the neighborhoods and communities surrounding our churches.

Winning confidence stories

Halifax, Nova Scotia—the Parker Street Food and Furniture Bank. The Parker Street Food and Furniture Bank, a project of the Halifax Seventh-day Adventist Church, has fed thousands and provided countless others with furniture, job training, and free computers for students to complete their homework. Other services include the creation of a fund for people who are in a temporary financial crisis. Melvin Boutilier (better known as Mel) is a member of the Halifax church and has been the driving force behind this merciful service to the church's community since 1983. The community service won the confidence and attention not only of the local community, but also of the Canadian nation—the work has received more than twenty recognitions from local governments and organizations.

In an interview with Adventist News Network, Mel explained that the Halifax church had been Ingathering for years. He recalled, "We were soliciting funds . . . and people would say, 'What are you doing in the community?' I'd mumble something about we're making an effort, but then we'd be gone and people wouldn't see us until the next year."

Mel brought his Ingathering concerns to the Halifax church, who decided to make him the Community Services leader. Mel's new role in the church led to the creation of the Parker Street Food Bank in a single-car garage in 1983, with no funds and a limited food source. This venture grew more rapidly than expected and also exposed the need for another addition—a furniture bank—which was inspired by a single mother in need because she and her child slept on a blanket on the floor. After a mattress was found for this mother and daughter, and recognizing that the need was great, a furniture bank was added in a donated warehouse in 1996. To expand the food bank to serve the clients better, after intense fund-raising, the organization purchased and renovated a warehouse in the inner city in 1999–2000. This building could accommodate both banks, providing greater efficiency.

On Sabbath morning, January 13, 2001, three months after moving into the new warehouse, Mel was informed, at church, that the building was on fire. When he and several friends arrived at the scene, they saw the fire department in the process of cutting holes in the roof, and smoke was pouring out the windows. The second floor was completely gutted, and there was severe smoke and water damage on the first floor. Mel knew that if the building was destroyed, the insurance would not be sufficient to rebuild. The initial major fund-raising campaign (for the purchase and renovations) was blessed with success, but those resources were exhausted.

However, God's resources are never exhausted, and He blessed the continuance of His work. Without any request from Mel, the media took on the challenge of raising funds for rebuilding; TV and radio stations and newspapers ran the story across Canada. The coverage was unusually wide for such an event in which there were no injuries or loss of life. Financial support from organizations, churches, businesses, and the public flowed in. There were many donations of construction materials and volunteer labor. The insurance company showed a remarkable interest in the situation and worked with the organization to the full extent of their contractual agreement and beyond. When you are there for the community, they are there for you!

The fire at first appeared to be a disaster but later turned into a blessing. The result was a redesigned building with more space for classrooms, plus updated electrical, plumbing, and security systems. During the building's restoration, another necessity surfaced—providing skills toward self-sufficiency. Classrooms were built for teaching office skills. In partnership with Nova Scotia Community College, the Skills Development Center was born in 2003 with the purchase of an adjacent building. This center has allowed many students to be trained in a variety of trades and assisted in obtaining employment. God has blessed this whole organization enormously; it has two two-story buildings, four trucks, and two thrift stores (as fund-raisers), all without any debt.

Optional prayer meetings and worship services at the food bank also care for the spiritual needs of clients. Some people have not only placed their confidence and trust in Jesus' followers at Halifax Seventh-day Adventist Church, but have also decided to put their confidence in Jesus, by following Him, and joining the church.[3]

Namibia wholistic evangelism reaches the previously unreachable. In Namibia, Africa, the Dorcas Society[4] and Adventist Men's Organization (AMO) of the Zambezi and Kavango East Regions planned and prepared for an outreach-centered "Dorcamo Rally" in the villages near Siya, twenty-five miles (forty kilometers) west of Rundu, the capital of Kavango East. The church members raised funds and gathered food, blankets, and clothing for the weeklong outreach effort into that particular community. Teams went out into the surrounding villages to assess the needs of the people. They visited with everyone available in the homesteads in the area of Siya—about a six-mile (ten-kilometer) radius from the campground where the Dorcamo Rally would be held. They prayed for the sick, administered basic remedies, and provided additional needed help.

When the evangelistic rally began, all the materials for circulation were brought to the assembly area and dispersed to the various teams for distribution. It was quite an eye-opener, as most of the materials were brand-new blankets and clothes, bought by the Dorcas and AMO members. Generally, one expects donations to be second-hand blankets and clothes, but, though living in similar conditions, they brought brand-new items.

Previously, when evangelistic meetings were held in this area, there was no interest. But after meeting the needs of the people, the Dorcamo group left twenty-six people with an appointed Global Mission pioneer. Doing evangelism Christ's way works! And falling in love with Jesus is an important part of wholistic restoration. When this happens to those whom we serve, there is cause for rejoicing (Luke 15:7).[5]

Winning confidence opens doors at a Catholic church in Colombia. Following Christ's method, the leaders of the Seventh-day Adventist Church in the Upper Magdalena Conference in Colombia and the Adventist Development and Relief Agency (ADRA) decided to join hands and work together. They motivated each church member, regardless of age, to donate a week to God during the Easter season, dedicating their time, talents, and resources to help communities, using the theme "Salvation and Service." More than five thousand volunteers responded. The leaders requested an interview with the department governor to explain to him their plan of a comprehensive assistance program. The governor was astonished to learn of the well-organized plan and deployment of talents, but replied, "Unfortunately, we have no money to do all this." "Mr. Governor, this is free," replied our leaders. The governor quickly called his secretary: "Come here, quick—before they repent." And there, he signed eighty-nine letters to city leaders, asking that each community open its doors during Easter to the Seventh-day Adventist Church and ADRA because "they have a plan that will benefit our communities. If anyone objects, provide them an escort." That week the miracles began in eighty-nine cities and communities. Several young people who came to serve Jesus in the city of Socorro interviewed the Catholic priest and cleaned and beautified the church cemetery. The community members watched in amazement as this army of volunteers joyfully did this work and other tasks for free. While the young people were not preaching, they were touching the hearts of many. Again they approached the priest and offered to paint the interior of the church for free, and they did. The priest was moved and told our youth, "This Easter I will shorten the Mass in order to allow you to use the church to present a message from Jesus every night." And so it happened; the soil was so well prepared by Christ's method, that there was no room in the church building for the large crowd that came. The youth placed the podium and the sound equipment at the doors of the church and talked every night to thousands of attendees who gathered in the square outside the church. Because Christ's method never fails, a door for preaching was opened. Since then, the conference follows the same plan every year with wonderful results.[6]

Again, why did large crowds follow Jesus?

This story of the large crowd in Colombia is reminiscent of Jesus' ministry: "Jesus went throughout Galilee, teaching in their synagogues, proclaiming the good news of the kingdom, and healing every disease and sickness among the people. News about him spread all over Syria, and people brought to him all who were ill with various diseases, those suffering severe pain, the demon-possessed, those having seizures, and the paralyzed; and he healed them. Large crowds from Galilee, the Decapolis, Jerusalem, Judea and the region across the Jordan followed him" (Matthew 4:23–25). Jesus won their confidence by His powerful, authoritative, and authentic teaching, preaching, and life. He formed relationships with people, sympathized with them, and met their wholistic needs. Today, many will follow Jesus if His disciples pursue His always-relevant ministry formula of mingling, showing sympathy, ministering to needs, and winning their confidence.

> Make a social capital map of all the individuals and/or organizations in your church's neighborhood who have confidence in your church and with whom you could possibly partner to serve your neighborhood or community. If you struggle to find anyone to list, think of specific ways to gain confidence on behalf of Jesus in your community—and then do it!

1. James Krile, *The Community Leadership Handbook: Framing Ideas, Building Relationships, and Mobilizing Resources* (Saint Paul, MN: Fieldstone Alliance Publishing Center, 2006), 123–129.

2. See Monte Sahlin, "CS 02 Community Assessment and Social Capital," Sabbath School and Personal Ministries Department, accessed October 5, 2015, http://www.sabbathschoolpersonalministries.org/cs-02-community-assessment-and-social-capital.

3. Adapted from Mark A. Kellner and Adventist News Network, "Canada: Adventist Volunteer Receives National Honor in Ottawa Ceremony," April 27, 2006, Adventist New Network bulletin, http://news.adventist.org/all-news/news/go/2006-04-27/canada-adventist-volunteer-receives-national-honor-in-ottawa-ceremony/1962/. Additional information for this story was supplied by Thelma Boutilier and the North American Division's Adventist Community Services.

4. "Dorcas Society" (otherwise known as Dorcas) is the original name given to the social ministries organization in the local Seventh-day Adventist Church. Even though this organization's name was changed to Adventist Community Services in 1972, some parts of the world have retained the "Dorcas" name.

5. Information for this story was provided by Eben E. Greeff, the head of Global Mission and the Sabbath School and Personal Ministries Department of the Namibia Conference; and Gideon Reyneke, the head of Adventist/Global Mission and the Sabbath School and Personal Ministries Department of the Southern Africa Union Conference.

6. Information for this story was provided by Robert Costa, the Ministerial Association associate of the General Conference.

Jesus Bade Them, "Follow Me"

It was all happening too fast for the disciples to keep up emotionally. This weekend had been bizarre; in fact, the whole previous week had rattled every presupposition the disciples possessed. They had witnessed Jesus' triumphal entry the previous Sunday and the cleansing of the temple from merchants and money changers, which raised their hopes of a royal takeover. They had noted with pride how the priests, who had challenged the authority of Jesus, trembled at the thought of arresting Him for fear of the people.

The disciples had cringed as Jesus revealed to them signs of the end and had listened soberly as Jesus shared with them parables about how to wait for the coming of His kingdom of glory. They were confused by Jesus' hints at the Passover meal about being killed and having His body broken and His blood spilled for them. And this last weekend had become a nightmare that they wished would end. The arrest, beatings, Crucifixion, and burial had been such a trauma to them that they could not stop trembling at the memory.

And now, wonder of wonders, Mary Magdalene brought news that Jesus had risen from the dead. They had witnessed the empty tomb. Then, fearing that the Jews would come after them, the disciples went to their "safe house" and locked the doors.

Then it happened! Even with the doors still locked, Jesus showed up in the room. Joy overwhelmed them as Jesus pronounced His well-recognized greeting, "Peace be with you!" (John 20:19). He showed them His scars and set them at ease in His presence. Then Jesus said again, "Peace be with you!" and He added, "As the Father has sent me, I am sending you" (verse 21). He then breathed on them, saying, "Receive the Holy Spirit" (verse 22).

Think of it! Following Jesus leads to being sent by Him to serve as He served His Father. The intimate communion that Jesus had with His Father will be the close communion that the Holy Spirit will mediate for all those whom Jesus sends. Just as Jesus obeyed and represented His Father's authority, we will be empowered to obey and represent the authority of Jesus. However, we must always remember that this author-ity is *His* authority. In fact, just before His ascension, Jesus made it clear: "All authority in heaven and on earth has been given to me. Therefore go and make disciples of all nations" (Matthew 28:18, 19).

It has been said that a disciple is one who has accepted Jesus as Savior and Lord and is becoming like Jesus as one follows Him in the real world. Becoming a disciple involves deepening people's relationship with Jesus; helping them to understand His Word, the Bible; equipping them to share Jesus' love and His Word with others; and then sending them out to seek and make other disciples—new followers of Christ.

Jesus' statement "follow Me" is not only for those outside the church, but also for those inside. Those who follow Jesus are not simply saying Yes to Him for the first time. Following Jesus is not just knowing the right doctrines and rejoicing that we are saved. We are saved to serve. Following Jesus is acting, responding, and doing ministry in His image. Let's visit some churches where this is happening.

The Aldergrove Seventh-day Adventist Church

One Sabbath morning, Dr. David Jamieson, the pastor of the Alder-grove Seventh-day Adventist Church in Aldergrove, British Columbia, Canada, gave an altar call during his "Kingdom Assignment" sermon series. This was a call to accept the kingdom assignment of Jesus by fol-lowing His ministry method of reaching people. Pastor Jamieson preached a sermon on the parable of the talents and invited his church members to come forward to receive one hundred dollars as seed money to do a kingdom assignment. Thirty different people came up that day to receive the hundred dollars and were challenged to multiply it to do an act of kindness outside the walls of the church, anywhere in the world. Pastor Jamieson's sermon series also issued two other challenges: some church members were asked to sell a treasure worth one hundred dollars or more and to give the proceeds toward a kingdom assignment project. The other was for each church member to give ninety minutes of their time during the designated three-month period to do acts of kindness.

This birthed Aldergrove's extensive AOK (Acts of Kindness) ministry. AOK shares twelve community initiatives, which are now funded by the community. The following are a few examples:

- Breakfast Club (providing a healthful breakfast in a local elementary school every day throughout the school year)
- Partnership with the Rotary Club to build a skateboard park for teens
- Providing a free oil and filter change with a car wash for single mothers twice a year
- Minivans for Moms (providing—free of charge—refurbished, roadworthy vehicles to single mothers whose current vehicles are ready to die)
- Giving money to foster community-based projects
- Restoring one house per year for a family in desperate need (Extreme Home Repair)

With the decision of many church members to follow Jesus in a deeper, more active, and practical way, many people in the community surrounding the church have decided to follow Jesus too. The Aldergrove Seventh-day Adventist Church has between 40 and 60 percent of its members engaged in community-based ministry, which has resulted in the church membership more than doubling in ten years (350 members to 825 members), with two services on Sabbath for Adventists and non-Adventists, or, better said, "pre-Adventists."

In August 2015, the Church in the Valley, a Seventh-day Adventist Church (formerly Aldergrove Seventh-day Adventist Church), opened a new church campus in neighboring Langley, British Columbia. This new campus houses a nine-hundred-seat worship center, an enlarged AOK center, and a youth center. Now they can make an even bigger AOK mark on their community!

As you can see from the membership growth of Church in the Valley, effective community-based ministries provide motivation for those who are being served to avail themselves of spiritual resources offered by the church. "The Saviour made each work of healing an occasion for implanting divine principles in the mind and soul. This was the purpose of His work. He imparted earthly blessings, that He might incline the hearts of men to receive the gospel of His grace."[1] This is the ultimate mission of the church—reaching the lost and preparing the people in and outside of our church for Christ's second coming.

Following Jesus in the city of Seven Lakes

The three Adventist churches in San Pablo City in the Laguna Province of the Philippines genuinely wanted to help their community and lead people to follow Jesus. After much prayer and discussion, the San Pablo church members decided to start with what little they had in their outreach fund—only sixty pesos.[2] First, they found a building to rent that they could use for an Adventist Community Services (ACS) center; the sixty pesos went to pay the rent for the first month.

The people in the San Pablo area were touched by the service the ACS center provided to them to meet their food and clothing needs. In April 2006, the church members held an evangelistic campaign at the ACS center. Twenty people chose to follow Jesus and were baptized at the end of these meetings.

The ministry of the San Pablo ACS center expanded. They started an Adopt-a-Barangay program (a *barangay* is a neighborhood). The ACS center offered medical-surgical services through health professionals who volunteered their time. Blood pressure screening services, weekly dental services, and aerobic exercise classes every Sunday were also included. Other services included retreats and Saturday night social gatherings for youth, healthful cooking classes, and a wedding ministry. The San Pablo churches offered their church buildings, their pastors, and other help for couples getting married so that they could have a quality wedding. Couples that normally could not afford it could now have a full-blown church wedding and reception.

In September 2006, the San Pablo church members held a second evangelistic meeting at the ACS center, using a health and family seminar format. This time, seventy-two souls accepted Christ and were baptized. Some of the newly baptized members formed a new company, the Lakeview Seventh-day Adventist Company. In six months, this company grew from 25 members to 140 members.

After two years of these community service activities, twelve barangays were entered; twelve Family & Health Seminars were held; four thousand people were served; one thousand souls were baptized; and five new congregations were planted. Proof yet again that "this work will not, cannot, be without fruit."[3]

Balance is needed

Balance is needed to keep churches from getting exclusively caught up in social ministries to the neglect of reaping. Though social ministry is extremely important, intentionally providing the people we serve with opportunities to follow Jesus is a crucial part of following Jesus' wholistic method of community transformation. The true restoration and transformation of communities only happens when Jesus regenerates the hearts of individuals within communities. Intentional opportunities from our churches toward this end could include Bible studies, small groups for discipleship, public reaping meetings, and church plants. Remember that it is better to plant a ministry first, and then grow a church out of that ministry. A study of forty-one denominations and faith groups, including Adventists, showed that "growing churches are very active in public evangelism, small-group evangelism, and personal evangelism. They are also very involved in community service. *The declining churches are the ones that eschew community service and focus entirely on evangelism, or eschew evangelism and focus entirely on community service.*"[4]

Community service is like testing and preparing soil in a field. Remember, your service attracts the people you meet in your community toward knowing Jesus and His Word. Small-group evangelism and personal evangelism (sharing your faith, giving out literature, giving Bible studies,[5] and so on) plant seed, which is the Word of God (Luke 8:11). Reaping occurs when people are invited to accept Jesus and His Word. Then intentional measures must be taken to preserve the harvest (making disciples). This could be continued Bible study and friendship support in small groups as well as individual nurturing relationships. For example, newly baptized people benefit from assigned mentors from their new church family; remember that all new members need at least six friends in the church to encourage them in their new lives in Jesus.

How about *your* church?

Are you following all of Christ's methods in reaching the people around you? As you meet their felt needs, there is a better chance they will discover they have another need they might not have felt before—Jesus!

Within God's kingdom, our fruit does not show immediately. Often one plants, another waters, and yet another one reaps (see John 4:37, 38). As your church meets people's felt needs, also plan to hold small groups, personal Bible studies, and regular reaping meetings, and follow up with an invitation to follow Jesus and His teachings and be baptized. And remember, preserving the harvest needs as much intentionality as the farming and reaping.[6] Following Jesus is an ongoing occupation that is to continue throughout a person's life. Jesus said, *"Remain* in me, as I also remain in you. No branch can bear fruit by itself; it must remain in the vine. Neither can you bear fruit unless you remain in me" (John 15:4; emphasis added).[7]

Small groups are an effective way to prepare people to follow Jesus and to keep them following Him for the rest of their lives. The following are various types of small groups.

Small groups for general Bible study for people you meet via community outreach programs. Gerson Santos[8] suggests a process for developing small groups from non-Adventists attending our community outreach programs: (1) Winsomely invite them to study the Bible to meet their spiritual needs. (2) Hold these groups at convenient times, such as during a lunch hour. (3) Do not teach a doctrinal series in these small groups—a person may join the group late and come for the first time during a study on the mark of the beast. Rather, do more generic Bible studies, such as the life of Jesus. The *Serendipity Bible*[9] is an example of a useful tool for leading general small groups. Small-group activities, icebreakers, and discussion questions are included with the words of Scripture. (4) If someone in the group asks questions about Bible doctrines, the group leader can say that after the program the inquirer can make an appointment for another day to study what the Bible teaches about the subject. A personal meeting with a person also can provide an opportunity to invite that person to accept Christ as his or her personal Savior before studying His doctrines (thematic teachings) in Scripture.[10] (5) There are many options for thematic Bible study lessons, such as Discover Bible guides, Amazing Facts Bible study guides, and Pillars of Faith (by Gerson Santos). What is the best lesson series? Pastor Santos says, "The best Bible study series is the one you use." (6) Those who are baptized should join a small group within your church, in members' homes, and so forth. If you do not already have small groups organized in your church, a good place to start is Sabbath School classes, which are small groups that already exist in your church. Small groups are not only for Bible study, but should have outreach projects, fun fellowship, and so on.

New members' Sabbath School class. The General Conference Sabbath School and Personal Ministries Department has developed a *New Members' Bible Study Guide* series, entitled *In Step With Jesus,* to assist in the task of making disciples. With fifty-two lessons, this series is a valuable resource for helping new members connect with church members and with God. It will help them to understand and follow God's Word, will demonstrate how to minister to others, and will equip them for discipleship during that all-important first year as church members.[11]

Regular Sabbath School classes. If your classes are large, you may want to consider dividing them into smaller groups. Each class should not only study the Bible, but have a care coordinator who organizes care and follow up for missing class members. Each class should also have a community outreach project.[12]

Generations of Christ followers

When we mingle, sympathize, minister to needs, win confidence, and then bid someone to follow Jesus, we invite them to mingle, sympathize, minister to needs, win confidence, and bid others to follow Jesus, thus producing new generations of followers of Christ and His method. Every step in the progression of Christ's method is success—not only the "follow Me" part. However, to fully follow Christ's ministry model, we must include all the steps and continue to disciple people after they say Yes to Jesus.

"Whoever claims to live in him must live as Jesus did" (1 John 2:6). "We need not go to Nazareth, to Capernaum, or to Bethany, in order to walk in the steps of Jesus. We shall find His footprints beside the sick-bed, in the hovels of poverty, in the crowded alleys of the great city, and in every place where there are human hearts in need of consolation. In doing as Jesus did when on earth, we shall walk in His steps."[13]

> Practice giving a gospel presentation to another person (see foot-note 10). Prayerfully be alert for opportunities to present the gospel to others.

1. Ellen G. White, *The Ministry of Healing,* 20.

2. Sixty Philippine pesos is equivalent to approximately $1.50 in U.S. money.

3. White, *The Ministry of Healing,* 143.

4. Monte Sahlin, *Adventist Congregations Today: New Evidence for Equipping Healthy Churches* (Milton-Freewater, OR: Center for Creative Ministry, 2003), 20.

5. Read the example of Philip giving Bible studies in Acts 8:26–40.

6. To access effective tools for discipling and keeping the people you reap, go to https://www.growingfruitfuldisciples.com.

7. Also see verse 16.

8. At the time of this writing, Gerson Santos was the director of the Urban Ministry Study Center, part of the Office of Adventist Mission.

9. *Serendipity Bible for Groups* (Littleton, CO: Serendipity House, 1988). Also available is *The NIV Serendipity Bible for Study Groups* (Grand Rapids, MI: Zondervan Publishing House, 1989).

10. For bringing individuals to Christ, Del Dunavant suggests using a gospel presentation that includes a "PSA" outline: (1) the *problem* of sin (Romans 3:23); (2) the *solution*—God's gift (Romans 6:23); (3) the individual must *accept* the gift (Ephesians 2:8, 9), praying a simple prayer, such as, "Dear Jesus, I realize I'm a sinner and deserve to die. I accept Your gift of eternal life. I want You to be my Lord and Savior. Thank You for Your gift. Amen." After that, make an appointment with that person to help him or her to fall in love with Jesus by establishing a Bible study and prayer life. Adapted from Del Dunavant, the director of Evangelism and Church Growth for the Northern California Conference.

11. Adapted from "In Step With Jesus," Sabbath School and Personal Ministries Department, accessed October 5, 2015, http://www.sabbathschoolpersonalministries.org/in-step-with-jesus.

12. The four focus points of Sabbath School are Bible study, fellowship, world mission emphasis, and community outreach.

13. White, *The Desire of Ages,* 640.

CHAPTER

Urban Ministry in
the End Time

A model of urban ministry

Various Adventist churches and institutions have demonstrated a balanced model of urban ministry: (1) missional church communities, (2) centers of influence, (3) small groups, and (4) ministry planting that becomes church planting.[1] The following are two examples—and we need many, many more.

Seoul Joong-ang Gospel Center

The Seoul Joong-ang Gospel Center is an urban church in the business district of Seoul, South Korea. Years ago, when Pastor Kim Dae Sung was the pastor of this Adventist congregation, he caught an idea from Ellen White's writings to have a vegetarian restaurant in his church's neighborhood. Before moving ahead, he chose to interview community leaders in his territory to determine whether *they* felt this idea would meet a real need, and, if so, whether they would support it.

Pastor Kim Dae Sung also visited the businesses around the church and explained his idea, asking for their input. From these interviews, he acquired pledges of support and money from them to start the restaurant, for they indicated that it would meet a real need. The neighborhood had many Buddhists and needed a good vegetarian restaurant for employees to have a place to eat during their lunch hour. The Buddhist temple across the street also wanted the restaurant, and they pledged their support and donated money.

Members of the Seoul Joong-ang Gospel Center started the vegetarian restaurant in their church building in 2002. They actually call it a vegetarian club. Restaurant customers pay in advance—like club dues. This center of influence[2] is open Monday through Friday; an ongoing goal is that it will continuously provide an opportunity for the church to connect with its community. Two hundred people eat at the vegetarian club each day. The church uses the income from the club to support the neighborhood, which makes the customers very happy. In addition to the good food, comprehensive health (physical, mental, and spiritual) resources, such as books and healthful foods, are available for the customers to buy. Several people have accepted Jesus and joined His church, by His grace, all because of this restaurant ministry.

Through the vegetarian club, the church has demonstrated the process of gospel farming: preparing the soil, planting seeds, and cultivating the resulting crop. The reaping part is especially illustrated in another of the Seoul Joong-ang Gospel Center's community-based ministries—their ministry to senior citizens.

A study of this region of the city showed that the church was located near a transportation hub of buses and trains. Because senior citizens have free rides on public transportation, many seniors pass by the church. The church responded to that reality and started a ministry for seniors.

The church has two separate worship services: one for seniors (downstairs) with approximately three hundred attendees, and one for other church members (upstairs) with approximately three hundred attendees. An associate pastor of the church is in charge of the senior citizen congregation.

On Sabbaths, the senior ministry looks like this: During Sabbath School time, a generic program is presented—generally an educational video on health. The worship service is from 10:00 to 11:00 A.M. From 11:00 to 11:30, four different kinds of activities are offered: (1) Bible study, (2) singing time (gospel music), (3) English class, and (4) health class. Then the seniors enjoy a delicious lunch in the vegetarian restaurant. In addition, on the first Sabbath of each month, there are free medical services (visits with a physician and the like) and beauty services (free haircuts, and so on). On the third Sabbath of each month, the church provides a variety of free injections.

Twice per year the church holds reaping meetings for those they minister to. The meetings are held after lunch four Sabbaths in a row during the reaping times, with baptisms on the fifth Sabbath. There are an average of ninety baptisms per year at Seoul Joong-ang Gospel Center—approximately eighty of which are from the senior citizens' group. The growing congregation for senior citizens continues to disciple the seniors who were baptized, and they have an ongoing Bible study class for new members.

Centers of influence

The Seoul Joong-ang Gospel Center is an example of a center of influence. More than one hundred years ago, Ellen White told church leaders that the church had neglected the cities. She recognized that there are certain classes of people who cannot be reached by public meetings. Thus, she counseled that "we should establish in all our cities small plants which shall be centers of influence."[3] Centers of influence are wholistic ministry centers, which connect church members with their communities and "place [them] where they will come in direct contact with those needing help."[4] "Through the social relations, Christianity comes in contact with the world."[5] These centers facilitate that vital contact.

Centers of influence were intended to feature a wide variety of activities, such as lifestyle education, treatment rooms, bookstores, reading rooms, vegetarian restaurants, literature ministries, lectures, small groups, instruction on preparing wholesome food, and more.[6] The activities of each center vary depending on an accurate assessment of local community needs.

The General Conference Office of Adventist Mission has given the center-of-influence concept a modern brand name: Life Hope Centers. As shown in the story from Seoul, centers of influence, or Life Hope Centers, are platforms on which Christ's method of ministry can be followed. Life Hope Centers can appear in many places, such as a local church, a rented facility, or a community center. They should be the result of teamwork between Adventist personnel, departments, services, and institutions. Life Hope Centers can offer a variety of contributions to your church's community: (1) *educating, equipping, and mentoring with seminars* on health, family, finance, microbusiness, technology, music lessons, language, and so forth; (2) *providing activities*—fitness, animal care, health screenings, community gardens, after-school care, hobby-based gatherings; (3) *events,* such as a community concert, health fair or expo, disaster preparedness and coordination, international food fairs, and so on; (4) *businesses* can be mission focused in the form of vegetarian restaurants, fitness centers, thrift shops, specialty shops, clinics, day-care centers; (5) a launching pad for various *community services*— food banks, clothing distribution, park cleanup, adult education and/or literacy, tutoring. Some community services may be generated by the center; others may be operated by other organizations, and the centers can contribute to or join them.

A key quality in Life Hope Centers is sustainability. Organizers need to plan for continuous interaction with the community in helpful Christian service and evangelistic outreach, rather than lapsing into sporadic activities.[7]

Bible study groups often spring from centers of influence/Life Hope Centers, because when the recipients of love and care are helped and healed, they often desire to meet the Healer. In the city of Jakarta, Indonesia, centers of influence—community health food stores in the city and outposts in the country—have brought their clients physical, mental, social, and spiritual healing. These centers have clearly introduced those they serve to the Healer.

Chinese Ministry Center

Many Chinese Buddhists in Indonesia converted to Christianity in 1997 during a financial crisis that hit Southeast Asia. In 2003, the Chinese Ministry Center in Jakarta (CMC) sprang out of the need to minister to this minority group.[8]

CMC uses health evangelism as its primary method for reaching out to its community and is effectively reaching upper-middle-class people. CMC's Club Sehat, a grocery store chain in Jakarta, is well known by Jakarta residents as a place to buy healthful food and to learn about a healthy lifestyle. By 2014, there were four Club Sehat stores, and three churches were generated in Jakarta by these stores. There is also a church in Surabaya, East Java. At the time of this writing, another new church was started in the outskirts of Jakarta. All of these churches have been planted as a direct result of Christ-centered health evangelism facilitated by CMC. Additionally, Bible study groups have played an important role in forming and strengthening these churches.

CMC also has a strong outpost ministry in the mountain area outside Jakarta. Three times per year CMC holds a health camp and a NEWSTART health retreat.[9] Various health seminars and cooking classes are also held at the CMC outpost. Here city dwellers receive help not only for their physical lives, but also for their spiritual lives.

Currently, a live-in lifestyle center, called Springs of Living Water, is being developed outside Jakarta; it will also serve as a community center. While living there, patients will participate in the NEWSTART program. Springs of Living Water will include an evangelism training center, a media center, and an organic farm.

CMC airs three radio talk shows that emphasize health and spiritual themes in addition to television health programs, which are especially geared to reach the city.

These media outreaches draw people to the four grocery stores. The country of Indonesia is truly being impacted with the gospel by these centers of influence.

Outpost centers

The outpost model, as exemplified by the grocery stores in the city of Jakarta and the retreat center in the mountains outside Jakarta, is presented repeatedly in Ellen White's writings. The following is one example: "Repeatedly the Lord has instructed us that we are to work the cities from outpost centers. In these cities we are to have houses of worship, as memorials for God, but institutions for the publication of our literature, for the healing of the sick, and for the training of workers, are to be established outside the cities."[10] Here it is clear that White emphasized the outpost model for institutions, but not in relation to local churches. At times, she also advocated that schools be established in the cities for those children who could not attend schools outside the cities. Typical of her balanced approach when dealing with issues, she wrote on the topic in terms of both the ideal and the practical.[11]

Several outposts have sprung up through the years as church-supportive health and educational ministries. Champions of this style of ministry, such as John Tindall and Wilmont "Bill" Frazee, have led the way. Outpost Centers International (OCI) networks and fosters Advent-ist supporting ministries around the world. This organized gospel out-reach is largely led by lay members and, along with some denomination-ally run outposts, complements the organized Seventh-day Adventist Church.

Historical vignettes of city work in the Adventist Church

Original Adventist city missions. In addition to a strong emphasis on the outpost model, the Seventh-day Adventist Church established city missions. The original city missions were established from 1883 to 1893. A General Conference report on city missions in 1886 indicated 36 city missions, 102 denominational workers, and 224 laypeople involved.

Urban medical missionary work. From 1897 to 1904, there was an emphasis on health and social work in the cities, along with Bible work-ers and evangelists. A famous example of a large, well-established city mission during that time was run by Dr. John H. Kellogg in Chicago.[12]

Ellen White was supportive of this mission in the beginning. How-ever, as the Chicago city mission progressed, Ellen White wrote to Dr. Kellogg, giving firm counsel addressing the fact that the mission was deliberately avoiding pointing its clients to Jesus.[13] Ellen White also referred to the work of the Salvation Army in her counsel to Kellogg. She said, "The Lord has marked out our way of working. As a people we are not to imitate and fall in with Salvation Army *methods*. This is not the work that the Lord has given us to do. . . . But the Lord has plainly pointed out the work that Seventh-day Adventists are to do. Camp meetings and tent meetings are to be held. The truth for this time is to be proclaimed. A decided testimony is to be borne."[14]

Some have used the above statement about Salvation Army methods as a rationale not to help the poor through social ministry. What were the Salvations Army's "methods"? In 1894, in an article in *Signs of the Times®*, Ellen White explained their methods:

We need to study methods whereby we may preach the gospel to the poor and downtrodden and degraded of humanity. *But let no one think that God will approve of a method which will require a man to act the part of a clown, or like a man who has lost his senses. Such methods as these are wholly unnecessary and inappropriate.*

Among the Salvation Army workers such methods as these have been employed; but it is more necessary that they should study and preach the word than act in a sensational way in order to draw the attention of the people.[15]

The same article also emphasizes the need for all Christians to help the poor. Here we see that we cannot merely jump to conclusions over one statement by itself but must consider what the Bible says and what Ellen White says elsewhere about the same issue.[16]

The Haskells' New York City mission. From 1900 to 1902, Stephen and Hetty Haskell lived in New York City and ran a mission there. They included medical programs as well as an emphasis on personal evangelism and witnessing.[17] The Haskells demonstrated that there are times when it is appropriate for families to work from within a city.[18] Ellen White placed much importance on the work in New York. She said that it was to be "a symbol of the work the Lord desires to see done in the world."[19] What does the "symbol" look like? The Haskells demonstrated it and so do all who follow Christ's wholistic ministry method.

Mandate and challenges of urban ministry

In these end times, the cities constitute the largest part of the uncompleted mission of the church. Generally speaking, the Seventh-day Adventist Church has been strongest in rural areas and islands. Yet, in a study of 107 periodical articles written by Ellen White, 24 articles provided instruction on moving or establishing institutions outside cities. But the remaining 75 percent give specific instruction to move into the cities to reach the people.[20]

To some, intense urban ministry might seem overwhelming. In cities, we find that many of the members of the church live in communities distant from the church. The pressures of making a living financially make it more difficult to get volunteers to invest time and effort beyond participating in Sabbath worship and possibly prayer meetings. A culture of individualism is more prevalent in urban centers. With crowding, there are personal safety issues that further isolate people from one another. Also, because of the reputation of cities, many people do not want to serve in such environments. There is concern that "our youth be shielded from the temptations of city life."[21]

Cities contain many cultures, ethnic groups, languages, religions, and needs—making it necessary to use different approaches to reach urban areas with the gospel.

We should not think of a city as one homogeneous unit. Cities, by nature, are composed of dozens or hundreds of subcommunities—each having its own gatekeepers (influential leaders who take it upon themselves to protect the identity of the neighborhood). If church members have not made efforts to connect with these subcommunities, they will be considered outsiders. To be considered an outsider usually makes it difficult or impossible for the church to have a transforming impact on the community. This and other realities may strike fear in the hearts and minds of those called to plant ministries in urban centers.

Urban phobia isn't new. The Bible, an urban Book,[22] shows that thousands of years ago, cities brought fear and discomfort to the hearts of certain people who were called to interact with cities. The stories of the spies sent by Moses (Numbers 13:17–33) and of God sending Jonah to Nineveh (Jonah 1–4) are examples of biblically recorded apprehension and disdain for cities.

Today, do not despair. We serve a God with a plan, and the battle is His! But the choice is ours: Do we approach the cities as Jonah did, who valued the comfort of his shade-producing vine more than God's gracious reprieve for the repentant masses of Nineveh? Or do we reflect God's heart for the cities and ask ourselves, *Should I not be concerned about that great city?* (see Jonah 4:11). What will it take for those of us who are outside the cities to value the grace of God in sending us in—over the comfort of the shade of our own fellowship?

Even if you do not live in a city, adopt a city in your region and plan with your church a way to connect with the gatekeepers (leaders) in one of the city's subcommunities so that you can meet a definite need there.

1. Adapted from Gerson Santos.

2. For a sample of Ellen White's counsel regarding centers of influence, see Ellen G. White, *Testimonies for the Church,* 7:112–115, and *Medical Ministry* (Mountain View, CA: Pacific Press® Publishing Association, 1932), 329.

3. White, *Testimonies for the Church,* 7:115.

4. White, *Testimonies for the Church,* 8:76.

5. White, *The Desire of Ages,* 152.

6. For example, in the late 1800s, Ellen White was excited about the Seventh-day Adventist churches in San Francisco and Oakland because of a wide range of services they were providing to the neighborhoods around their churches. She called these two churches the "two beehives." They were centers of influence through many different endeavors. See Ellen G. White, "Notes of Travel—No. 3: The Judgments of God on Our Cities," *The Advent Review and Sabbath Herald,* July 5, 1906, 7.

7. This information was provided by Gary Krause and the General Conference Office of Adventist Mission.

8. "Profile: Chinese Ministry Center Jakarta," Outpost Centers International, accessed October 5, 2015, http://www.outpostcenters.org/ministry/cmc-jakarta/.

9. NEWSTART stands for Nutrition, Exercise, Water, Sunlight, Temperance, Air, Rest, and Trust in divine power. For more information on the NEWSTART program, go to http://newstart.com/.

10. Ellen G. White, *Country Living* (Washington, DC: Review and Herald® Publishing Association, 1946), 31.

11. George R. Knight, "Another Look at City Mission," *Adventist Review,* December 6, 2001, 27.

12. Monte Sahlin, *Mission in Metropolis: The Adventist Movement in an Urban World* (Milton-Freewater, OR: Center for Creative Ministry, 2007), 8.

13. For more background on this issue, see Richard W. Schwarz, *John Harvey Kellogg, M.D.* (Nashville, TN: Southern Publishing Association, 1970), 170ff.

14. White, *Testimonies for the Church,* 8:184, 185; emphasis added.

15. Ellen G. White, "The Missionary's Pattern," *Signs of the Times®,* March 19, 1894; emphasis added.

16. For example, consider the overall ministry patterns of Jesus as portrayed in Scripture; in White, *The Desire of Ages,* 637; and in many of Ellen White other writings.

17. Sahlin, *Mission in Metropolis,* 9.

18. See Ellen G. White, *Christian Service* (Washington, DC: Review and Herald® Publishing Association, 1925), 180.

19. Ellen G. White, *Evangelism* (Washington, DC: Review and Herald® Publishing Association, 1946), 385.

20. Sahlin, *Mission in Metropolis,* 16.

21. White, *Country Living,* 31.

22. Former professor of Mission at Andrews University, Bruce Moyer, points out that the Bible is an urban Book, which mentions 119 cities, closing with "the Holy City" (Revelation 21:2). For more information see, https://www.ministrymagazine.org/archive/2004/05/toward-a-theological-basis-for-urban-ministry.html.

CHAPTER

How Shall We Wait?

Injured and waiting

Our injured planet has been groaning and waiting to be restored for a long time. How shall we wait? Patiently, passionately, proactively (Romans 8:22–25; Matthew 24:36–25:46).

Waiting patiently and the kingdom of heaven

The theme statement of the Sixtieth General Conference Session of the Seventh-day Adventist Church (2015) was "Arise! Shine! Jesus Is Coming!" This triumphant announcement of the "blessed hope—the appearing of the glory of our great God and Savior, Jesus Christ" (Titus 2:13) is a significant part of the "everlasting gospel" (Revelation 14:6, KJV). However, while we wait for that blessed hope—that blessed certainty— we live in the world of the here and now, the world of the not yet. This liminal existence is similar to what Victor Turner calls the "betwixt-and-between period."[1]

In His prayer, Jesus said, "Thy kingdom come, Thy will be done in earth, as it is in heaven" (Matthew 6:10, KJV). His prayer is in the present tense and in the forever tense (verse 13). Kingdom values must happen *now* before His second coming, and they will continue through-out eternity. While we wait for His coming, His church must position itself to foster heaven on earth—*now*!

In *The Great Controversy,* Ellen White portrays the kingdom of God in two parts: "the kingdom of grace" and "the kingdom of glory."[2] Because "the end is not yet" and we still await the kingdom of glory, we must arise and shine now and concern ourselves with kingdom living and actions that share God's love and grace (Matthew 24:6, KJV).

"Social action is a living witness to our soon-returning Lord. When we take a stand for justice, compassion, and healing, we demonstrate the values of the coming Kingdom."[3] In southern Africa, Patricia demonstrates kingdom values as she lovingly cares for nearly twenty children in her home who have contracted AIDS or have lost their parents to AIDS. When asked why she does this, she replied, "I want them to have a little bit of the Second Coming now."[4]

Waiting and the end-time remnant

Because God's kingdom of grace *has come* and His kingdom of glory *will come*—we must *go*! Even though we wait patiently (Romans 8:25), we must wait proactively—not as spiritual introverts, but as spiritual extroverts. God's end-time, remnant church members must not allow their identity as "the remnant" to foster an exclusive-truth attitude that alienates their congregations from communities (Revelation 12:17, KJV). In his devotional, *The Chosen*, Dwight Nelson further warns that the opposite attitude is just as mistaken. In an effort to be accepted by and not to offend the communities outside our churches, church members must not make the mistake of forgetting that we are "a chosen people," called by God to "declare the praises of him who called [us] out of darkness into his wonderful light" (1 Peter 2:9).[5] Being a chosen *remnant* raises the question, Of what are we "the remnant"? It implies that we are part of and must continue what was before our time—the incarnational presence and ministry that Jesus lived when He started His church on earth.

One of the characteristics of the remnant people is that they keep God's commandments, including the fourth commandment in the Decalogue (Revelation 12:17). The Sabbath will be the context of the great test of loyalty to God at the end of time.[6] It is and will be "an evidence of loyalty to the Creator."[7] Additionally, Matthew 25:31–46 makes it clear that caring for the needs of others is also an end-time test. Do you see any relationship between these two end-time tests: the Sabbath and caring for the needs of others? Are they different tests, or are they parts of one test? Could they be two aspects of that end-time test of loyalty to God?

The judgment scene in Matthew 25 is a test of the Sabbath attitude as explained in Isaiah 58. "Whether or not we keep the Sabbath *and* care for the needy will reveal the status of our relationship with Jesus— our loyalty to Him and our willingness to make Him and His earthly family a priority. They both are about how we treat Jesus, who will say, 'Truly I tell you, just as you did it [or did not do it] to one of the least of these who are members of my family, you did it [or did not do it] to me' (Matthew 25:40, NRSV; compare verse 45)."[8]

Waiting and eschatology

The Seventh-day Adventist Church has always been an eschatological movement; part of this responsibility, as noted earlier, is caring for others. On Judgment Day, "the defining question will not be, 'Did you *know* the truth?' " Rather, as noted in *Pursuing the Passion of Jesus,* it will be, " 'Did you *show* the truth?' "[9] "When the nations are gathered before Him, there will be but two classes, and their eternal destiny will be determined by what they have done or have neglected to do for Him in the person of the poor and the suffering."[10] Orthodoxy without orthopraxy (correctness or orthodoxy of action or practice)[11] is not enough. "The world will be convinced, not by what the pulpit teaches [orthodoxy], but by what the church lives [orthopraxy]. The minister in the desk announces the theory of the gospel; the practical piety of the church demonstrates its power."[12]

Paradise Valley Seventh-day Adventist Church—demonstrating practical piety while waiting

The first angel in Revelation 14:6 proclaims the everlasting gospel "to every nation, tribe, language and people." Paradise Valley Seventh-day Adventist Church, formerly a dying congregation outside of San Diego, California, is taking this end-time message very seriously. They have a powerful ministry that demonstrates the gospel to immigrants from many nations.

After conducting an assessment of their neighborhood, the Paradise Valley church discovered the need for the establishment of a food bank. Soon after the recent economic recession began, they were blessed with the donation of a walk-in cooler from a florist who was going out of business. This gave birth to their food ministry. Soon the food bank ministry was thriving. Food was sorted, bagged, and distributed every Tuesday to residents of their community. In 2011, they collected and gave away more than 425,000 pounds (192,777 kilograms) of fresh produce and perishable food and well over 15,000 pieces of clothing with a value of more than $785,000! In addition, they hold a rummage sale twice a year that sells myriads of household and furniture items inexpensively.

From this ministry, they discovered that there are more than ninety thousand refugees living in the San Diego area, struggling to survive. By reaching out through their food ministry, they soon had refugees requesting to attend their church. The first group was a group of Bhutanese refugees who had fled Bhutan fifteen years before and had been living in squalor in refugee camps in Nepal since that time. These Hindu people had recently arrived in the United States, and they hungered to learn about the Christian God. Because they spoke no English, the church leadership had difficulty when attempting to tell them about Jesus—but this frustration gave birth to yet another Community Services ministry: the Refugee Assimilation Project (RAP) ministry. As part of this program, they established an English language school designed to reach the preliterate refugees who were coming to the Adventist church for assistance. Church buses pick up men and women for the language classes and pick up the refugees for Sabbath School and the worship service on Sabbath.

The Paradise Valley Community Services recognized that these refugees were required to have work experience in addition to English as a second language (ESL) classes in order to receive food stamps and medical insurance from the government. Refugees are required to spend a minimum of thirty-five hours a week split between ESL and work experience. The church leased a small building and established a thrift store to provide work experience for some of the refugees taking ESL. In its first four months, the Paradise Valley Thrift Store generated fifteen thousand dollars in gross income, or almost four thousand dollars per month—nearly repaying the start-up costs.

In addition, some students are helping them to develop a twelve-thousand-square-foot parcel of ground they have leased for a community garden. This provides construction skills for the students as they build garden boxes and prepare the ground for planting. The garden gives the community and refugee families a piece of land to grow their favorite foods, serving as a natural antidepressant for them. Still others help with the landscaping work around the church as well as custodial work each afternoon, to obtain a variety of work experiences.

The Paradise Valley church soon discovered the need for a good-quality child development center for the children of the refugees and others in the local area. The Child Development Center provides a safe place for refugee children and yet another area of work experience for the refugees.

More than 125 volunteers are active in Paradise Valley church ministries, and the list grows longer each month. The ministries continue to expand, providing other services, such as health-screening programs for the community with student nurses who volunteer their time.

Paradise Valley Seventh-day Adventist Church is baptizing more than sixty people per year without traditional evangelistic meetings. Within five years, more than 250 people have become church members. Refugees from as many as fifty different nationalities and ethnicities attend the worship service each Sabbath. The church provides translation in Arabic, French, Spanish, Laotian, Swahili, and Tagalog. They have two English language Sabbath School classes as well![13]

Waiting and end-time disasters, wars, pestilences . . .

So, how is the Seventh-day Adventist Church responding to end-time signs and troubles (Matthew 24:6–9)? Whenever there are major disasters, such as floods, earthquakes, hurricanes, and various pestilences, the Adventist Development and Relief Agency (ADRA) is there to bring relief and to help the victims rebuild their lives. ADRA works primarily outside of North America and has responded to high-profile disasters such as 2008's Cyclone Nargis in Myanmar, the various typhoons in the Philippines, the massive 2010 earthquake in Haiti, the Ebola outbreak in West Africa in 2014—the list is endless.[14]

In the North American Division (NAD), disaster response is primarily carried out by Adventist Community Services (ACS) Disaster Response.[15] For example, when the deadly Hurricane Katrina hit the Gulf region of the United States in 2005, ACS Disaster Response was at disaster sites, collaborating with national and local disaster response organizations by operating the materials distribution centers and bringing relief and restoration (ADRA was also at disaster scenes). Thirty-seven families returned to their rebuilt homes, thanks to the efforts of NAD ACS.

In late August 2011, Hurricane Irene pounded the Caribbean and the East Coast of the United States. After Irene roared through the state of New Jersey, the First Seventh-day Adventist Church of Paterson in New Jersey distributed relief goods for two days to the victims in the church's community. Because one of those days was Sabbath, Barack Obama, the president of the United States, who was surveying the damage in their community, told the Paterson church volunteers that he thought as Seventh-day Adventists they would be in church worshiping. Pastor David King replied that they *were* worshiping because "service is worship."

Waiting and the final harvest

The end of the world will be catastrophic and glorious all at the same time. This world has continually received foretastes of this final catastrophe. One of the glorious parts is that the end is pictured as a harvest (Matthew 13:39).

All harvests are a result of patient and conscientious farming. If we merely have events in our church program that are not part of an intentional process of "gospel farming," we are "Seventh-day Event-ists."[16] This approach is not likely to produce an abundant harvest that Jesus will come to gather at His second advent.

Below is a summary of some gospel-farming stages we have discussed in this book, formatted into "Ten Farming Commandments":

1. You shall study Jesus' ministry method[17] and pray for a spirit of love, respect, and caring for the people in your community; for the farmers and reapers in the harvest field; and for the rain—the Holy Spirit—throughout the growing season, until the final harvest (Matthew 13:39). No rain—no crop and harvest!
2. You shall assess the resources in thy church.
3. You shall establish a social action leadership team (SALT)—a core team who will help lead your church into making a differ-

ence where it is located.

4. You shall choose thy territory. Narrow it down.

5. You shall conduct a demographic analysis on the chosen territory.

6. You shall drive or walk around the chosen territory and note the types of homes, stores, churches, people, and so forth. (Also, do a prayer walk or drive, praying for those or what you see.)

7. You shall talk to community leaders and businesspeople to discover community needs as they see them.

8. You shall earn social capital. Join community boards, town councils, local ministerial associations (pastors), civic clubs, and the like to network with community leaders and businesspeople.

9. You shall develop a church strategic-ministry plan for the church's community involvement, based on the wholistic (physical, mental, social, and spiritual) community needs thou hast discovered and the resources and vision of thy church members for inside and outside the church. Then follow it!

10. You shall look for ways that God is already working in thy community. Celebrate, acknowledge, and collaborate. Get involved with local community service organizations and socialize with their personnel whenever possible.

And a bonus!

11. You shall not ignore commandments 1 through 10, and you shall remember to *reap* where you have farmed! (As the Spirit guides you, invite people to follow Jesus and attend seasonal reaping meetings, Bible studies, small groups, and so forth.) *Keep* whom you *reap* (disciple—preserve the harvest [John 15:16]), so that they may be gathered in the final harvest at the end of the world.[18]

Waiting and revival and reformation

God needs revived churches that have experienced reformation in their attitudes toward the lost. Revival and reformation are also about God cleansing our personal and corporate lives from sin (Psalms 139:23, 24; 51:10–12). Read the story of Jesus cleansing the temple in Matthew

21:12–15. What do we need to throw out of our church so that the poor, suffering, and afflicted ones will feel welcome and receive healing? Self-centeredness must go! Instead, our churches need members who are outward-focused, serving the community outside the church walls as well as those within. This attitude will revive and reform us and, by God's grace, bring revival and reformation to those we serve.

In *Autopsy of a Deceased Church: 12 Ways to Keep Yours Alive,* Thom Rainer presents his study of deceased churches in the United States. As he enumerated the reasons of their demise, a major cause repeatedly was mentioned: the churches that were dying or had already died disconnected from and stopped serving their communities. Their inward focus and self-serving killed them.[19]

Waiting and working

While we wait for Jesus' second coming, God is waiting too. He is waiting for us to quit waiting passively. "And start working."[20] "The last rays of merciful light, the last message of mercy to be given to the world, is a revelation of His character of love. . . . The light of the Sun of Righteousness is to shine forth in good works."[21]

If the soil in your community is like the problematic soils in Matthew 13, it's time to get to work and prepare more good ground while there is still time. "Merely to preach the Word is not ministry."[22] The fact is that some people in our fields can't be reached by conventional preaching evangelism. They need other connecting points. This book has endeavored to highlight that "old-time religion" that Jesus modeled.

The stories of Adventist churches and organizations that are community- and neighborhood-transforming agents continue to come in. Young children in Singaporean churches are involved in ACS's Pay It Forward movement, visiting homes with their adult mentors, bringing needed supplies, health tests, education, and the love of Jesus. Adventist-laymen's Services & Industries partners with local conferences of the Seventh-day Adventist Church, the Adventist Health System, and other entities to hold megaclinics in various cities, providing free health care for thousands. The Mowbray Seventh-day Church in Cape Town, South Africa, cleans a local train station and puts flowers there. The Maranatha Seventh-day Adventist Church in Brooklyn, New York, in partnership with other faith groups, civic leaders, public schools, and nonprofits, organizes an annual rally against gun violence, entitled "Bridging the Gap Between Church and Community." In Indonesia, community services range from providing coffins to comfort stations (and many things in between); one example, the Waingapu church in West Indonesia, in partnership with the villagers, built "comfort rooms" with toilets and showers in a village that had none, held evangelistic meetings in the evenings, and saw many souls accept Jesus and get baptized during the building project. Several Seventh-day Adventist schools at all levels have service days when students go out into the community to do acts of kindness. Neighborhood women from low-income families come at defined times to the Seventh-day Adventist church in Baku, Azerbaijan, to wash their clothes in washing machines in the church; while they wait, church members winsomely tell them about Jesus and His Word. What is your church's story? Is your church part of your community's story?

The answer is up to you, for you are the church. Empowered by Christ and His ministry methods, you and your church can and will make a difference!

> Once each year have your church do an evaluation of its ministry to ensure that the church is in tune with the wholistic ministry described in this book. Continue this cycle until Jesus comes.

---

1. Victor W. Turner, "Betwixt and Between: The Liminal Period in *Rites de Passage*," in *Symposium on New Approaches to the Study of Religion: Proceedings of the 1964 Annual Spring Meeting of the American Ethnological Society*, ed. June Helm (Seattle: American Ethnological Society, 1964), 4–20.

2. See Ellen G. White, *The Great Controversy* (Mountain View, CA: Pacific Press® Publishing Association, 1950), 346, 347.

3. Adventist Community Services International, *Keys to Adventist Community Services* (Lincoln, NE: AdventSource, 2008), 6.

4. Charles Sandefur, " 'A Little Bit of the Second Coming Now,' " *Ministry*, July 2009, 19–21.

5. Dwight K. Nelson, *The Chosen* (Hagerstown, MD: Review and Herald® Publishing Association, 2011), 46.

6. See White, *The Great Controversy,* 605.

7. Ibid.

8. May-Ellen Colón, *From Sundown to Sundown: How to Keep the Sabbath ... and Enjoy It!* (Nampa, ID: Pacific Press® Publishing Association, 2008), 155.

9. Nelson, *Pursuing the Passion of Jesus,* 26; emphasis in the original.

10. White, *The Desire of Ages,* 637.

11. *Dictionary.com,* s.v. "orthopraxy," accessed October 29, 2015, http://dictionary .reference.com/browse/orthopraxy?s=t.

12. White, *Testimonies for the Church,* 7:16.

13. For more information on Paradise Valley, as well as other thrilling stories of Adventist churches making a difference, see Bettina Krause, *It's Time: Stories From the Frontlines of Urban Mission* (Nampa, ID: Pacific Press® Publishing Association, 2015).

14. A statement from ADRA's fund-raising materials for May 10, 2014: "Acts of God are not found in the storm but in the response. Be an act of God." See http://ccadra.convio.net /trinet/dfro_2014/DFRO-Poster-WebEng.pdf.

15. Adventist Community Services is the Adventist social ministry organization that works out of the local church, whereas ADRA is the official nongovernmental organization sponsored by the Seventh-day Adventist Church to provide international relief and development. See Adventist Community Services International, *Keys to Adventist Community Services,* 13.

16. From a conversation with Celeste Ryan Blyden, vice president for Strategic Planning and Public Relations and director of Communication for the Columbia Union Conference.

17. White, *The Ministry of Healing,* 143.

18. Adapted from May-Ellen Colón, "How to Be a Good Farmer—Even in a City," *Elder's Digest,* January–March 2011, 27–29.

19. Thom S. Rainer, *Autopsy of a Deceased Church: 12 Ways to Keep Yours Alive* (Nashville, TN: B & H Publishing, 2014).

20. Nelson, *Pursuing the Passion of Jesus,* 11.

21. Ellen G. White, *Christ's Object Lessons* (Washington, DC: Review and Herald® Publishing Association, 1941), 415, 416.

22. White, *Ministry to the Cities,* 70.